"This publication makes a highly original and innovative contribution to grief studies—it explores the sometimes-neglected themes of subjective spiritual intimacy with one who is deceased."
—BERNADETTE FLANAGAN
Professor of Spirituality, South East Technological University

"*Growing Through Grief* is a wise, compassionate, and ultimately hopeful exploration of spirituality in widowhood. Buckingham shows us that the death of a spouse or life partner, though painful, can be a pruning for a greater flowering in later life. This book is a valuable guide which will be of help both to widows and to those accompanying them pastorally and spiritually. It is profoundly life- and love-affirming, for which the author deserves our gratitude."
—SOLINE HUMBERT
Author of *A Divine Calling*

"In the 1960s spirituality took a democratic turn. Now what was happening in every state of life and in the stages of everyone's life from childhood to old age was worthy of attention. Margery Buckingham illustrates this welcome development in the field with her fine book written with a spirituality lens about her life as a widow and her study of the lives of other widows."
—MICHAEL O'SULLIVAN, SJ
Director, Spirituality Institute for Research and Education

"Margery Buckingham brings not only her experience of widowhood but also her background in architecture to this book! The section on visualizing the process of grief resolution is especially interesting and makes an important contribution to the literature on bereavement."
—ANNE WINCHELL SILVER
Former Director, Center for Christian Spirituality,
The General Theological Seminary

Growing Through Grief

Growing Through Grief

Widowhood as a Catalyst for Spiritual Development

MARGERY MORGAN BUCKINGHAM

WIPF & STOCK · Eugene, Oregon

GROWING THROUGH GRIEF
Widowhood as a Catalyst for Spiritual Development

Copyright © 2026 Margery Morgan Buckingham. All rights reserved. Except for brief quotations in critical publications or reviews, no part of this book may be reproduced in any manner without prior written permission from the publisher. Write: Permissions, Wipf and Stock Publishers, 199 W. 8th Ave., Suite 3, Eugene, OR 97401.

Wipf & Stock
An Imprint of Wipf and Stock Publishers
199 W. 8th Ave., Suite 3
Eugene, OR 97401

www.wipfandstock.com

PAPERBACK ISBN: 978-1-6667-8314-8
HARDCOVER ISBN: 978-1-6667-8315-5
EBOOK ISBN: 978-1-6667-8316-2

VERSION NUMBER 031126

Scripture quotations marked CSB have been taken from the Christian Standard Bible®, Copyright © 2017 by Holman Bible Publishers. Used by permission. Christian Standard Bible® and CSB® are federally registered trademarks of Holman Bible Publishers.

Quotation from T. S. Eliot, *Four Quartets*, reprinted by permission of Faber and Faber Ltd.

To my daughter, Julia Marie Mason

With love and gratitude

Only through great love or great suffering do we access the greatest spiritual teachings.

—Richard Rohr

Contents

Acknowledgments | ix
Abbreviations | xi

Chapter 1
Was I Unique? | 1

Chapter 2
Spirituality | 10

Chapter 3
Widowhood | 23

Chapter 4
Grief | 30

Chapter 5
Spiritual Development | 41

Chapter 6
The Widows Speak | 46

Chapter 7
After-Death Communication | 58

Appendix
How Friends and Family Can Help | 67

Bibliography | 71

Acknowledgments

WITHOUT THE SUPPORT AND encouragement of Bernadette Flanagan, Soline Humbert, and Anne Silver, this book would not have been written. Thank you also to Cecilia DiBella, Robin Higgins, Kathleen Milster, Rose Richards, and Louise Woodruff for reading, critiquing, and making suggestions that improved the work. Gratitude also goes to the five American widows whose candor, honesty, and willingness to be interviewed opened my eyes and expanded my vision on this journey of widowhood.

Abbreviations

GTS   General Theological Seminary of the Episcopal Church
NDE   Near-Death Experience
SETU   South East Technological University
VISTA Volunteers in Service to America
VSCD   Vécus Subjectifs de Contact avec un Défunt (subjective experiences with a deceased)

Chapter 1

Was I Unique?

THREE YEARS AFTER MY husband of thirty-three years died of pulmonary fibrosis, I enrolled in a master's degree program in spiritual direction at the General Theological Seminary (GTS) of the Episcopal Church in New York City. This fulfilled a lifelong desire to study philosophy and theology beyond the undergraduate level. During those wonderful years of living in an academic and spiritual community, I began to wonder if my experience of spiritual growth was in any way related to becoming a widow. As we all live longer and women continue to outlive their male contemporaries, the understanding and support of widows becomes even more important for society.

Within a two-year period I had lost three people who were very dear to me: my husband, my mother at age ninety-six, and my best friend. Each death was prolonged through terminal illness. I was physically and emotionally exhausted by these experiences. My identity was shaken. Who was I now? What was I meant to do next?

Through much prayer and soul searching I was led to attend General Seminary, where I pursued a certificate in spiritual direction. I loved everything about that year—my classes, the assignments, the rhythm of the day that revolved around morning and evening chapel, the wonderful sense of community, and living in

Manhattan. Another year would allow me to complete a master's degree, but it was very expensive, and do people really choose a spiritual director based on a resume? I didn't think so. After graduating, however, my work was more with groups, both in spiritual direction and in leading retreats and quiet days. In my desire to expand my potential audience, I came to believe that the extra credential would be useful.

I also had a very personal reason for wanting to earn a master's degree. I spent many years in school, but still didn't have that degree. Instead I had two bachelor's degrees, the first taking four years and the second taking five years. At that point I was only four courses and a final project away from achieving that lifelong goal. So I went back for an additional year.

The second year was more difficult primarily because of the COVID-19 pandemic. All the classes became hybrid so that students could choose to stay safe at home rather than coming to campus. I did have a room and it was even better than the one I had my first year. This one had a kitchenette with a mini refrigerator and a microwave. During my first year I had kept milk and yogurt on the windowsill in the winter months.

Some of the hybrid classes were successful, but some were very disappointing. Senior faculty were not accustomed to teaching online. They would just display their typed lecture notes on the screen and read from them. Unfortunately, the only philosophy course the school offered was taught this way. Additionally, the teachers in that class got so bogged down that we never got beyond Descartes historically and never reached a discussion of logical positivism or other more contemporary theories. When I was an undergraduate I had eight semesters of mandatory philosophy at my Jesuit university and had taken the GTS course hoping to discover what had developed in the fifty years since then.

Another challenge of that second year was the required thesis. Luckily my mentor and head of the spiritual direction program had said, "You will do a project and I will be your advisor." With her approval I co-facilitated a six-month group spiritual direction program with a dozen homeless people in downtown Boston. That worked well, and I completed all the requirements for the master's degree in spiritual direction.

I loved being back in school, but further study at General Seminary wasn't ideal. The advanced curriculum was geared toward ordained clergy. Finding an appropriate overseas institution would give me a home base in Europe from which to travel. I also loved the idea of immersing myself in another culture. My French and Spanish were at the tourist level, so finding an English-speaking university became paramount. I had visited the University of Cork on an earlier trip to Ireland and found it intriguing, so I began on that website. While browsing I stumbled on an advertisement for a program in applied spirituality through Waterford Institute of Technology. The description was enticing, but I worried that the curriculum might be redundant after my most recent degree. Again Dr. Anne Silver, my advisor, friend, and mentor, came to my rescue. She reviewed the course descriptions, assured me of their relevance, and stressed that the emphasis on writing was something that I needed.

So I moved to Dublin, Ireland, found student accommodation with some difficulty, and began another year of study. For my research dissertation I formulated the question, "Under what circumstances does widowhood become a catalyst for spiritual development?" To answer this question I reviewed the existing literature on grief, widowhood, and the spiritual development of mature women. I also interviewed other widows about their experiences around the death of their spouse and how they navigated the aftermath. After nine months of intense reading and writing, my study concluded that spiritual development happens for a widow when:

1. The woman had an active spiritual life before her bereavement.
2. She has a supportive network of friends, family, or church groups.
3. She refocuses the energy she previously focused on her marriage into other creative, artistic, and spiritual areas.

In retrospect I can surmise that this refocus of available energy was something that I had experienced but didn't recognize at the time. My husband died in early December. The following spring I noticed that something was different. It wasn't just that he wasn't there. I realized that pulmonary fibrosis was no longer the center of my life as it had been after Bill's diagnosis. While he was sick we had an oxygen concentrator in our home and Bill wore an oxygen mask at all times except when he was in the shower, shaving, or eating. He even wore it while he was sleeping. He also had a portable concentrator that he took to work, to church, and on airplanes. The hum of the machines became the soundtrack of our lives.

In addition to the ubiquitous machines, there were doctor's appointments and daily medicine. At one point, when he had lost so much weight that he was technically malnourished, he was eating six meals a day. This meant that we were always either grocery shopping, cooking, or cleaning up. Because the medication he was taking made Bill immunosuppressed, the pulmonologist forbade him from riding the subway, which was his usual means of commuting to work. For several months this meant my spending four hours a day in the car driving him to and from work. Eventually we bought a second car, but the cost of in-town parking and his natural frugality prevented Bill from driving five days a week. The compromise was that he worked at home on Wednesdays, drove himself on Tuesday and Thursday, and I drove him on Monday and Friday. Luckily I had retired from my full-time job and only had to juggle my volunteer commitments in order to do this. To repeat, the cloud of terminal pulmonary fibrosis colored every aspect of our lives for the eighteen months from the initial diagnosis to Bill's ultimate death. When that cloud lifted I needed to adjust to a new normal.

I felt a need to redefine myself as someone other than a wife or widow. One of the first things I did was sell our house in one of the Boston neighborhoods and move to a one-bedroom condominium on the water in Onset, a small village on the south coast of Massachusetts.

Was I Unique?

Water had always been important to me. My earliest memory is of splashing in shallow water at the beach during the summer. When I was growing up, my family spent much time at a summer house belonging to a relative, often in the company of numerous cousins. Those were happy times and fond memories. In addition, water for me symbolizes nourishment, refreshment, cleansing, and renewal. Of course, water has all kinds of scriptural and spiritual associations. At one point Bill and I lived on the banks of the Neponset River. Daily we crossed a bridge a short distance from a waterfall that created rushing currents downstream. As I walked past I was often reminded of the words from Scripture "where streams of living water flow" (John 7:38 CSB).

The river wasn't enough water for me. In my opinion, if it isn't salt and tidal it doesn't count. I longed for the ocean. Bill grew up in Montana, a vast, landlocked western state. He didn't understand about the pull of the ocean for me. Sometimes I think there are mountain people and there are ocean people. I am definitely the latter. In the late eighties when we were living in Philadelphia, which is on the Delaware River, I had a visceral need to see the ocean. I put our son David in the car (Bill was in Boston for the weekend) and drove one hour to the nearest beach, which was Atlantic City, New Jersey. We walked along the shore, got an ice-cream cone, and drove back to Philadelphia, renewed and ready to continue our city life.

Bill and I had done a lot of traveling during our marriage. After he died I worried that those days were over. Was I ready and able to travel alone? I spent six months planning in order to spend one month in France by myself, despite having only high school French and a Duolingo refresher. Google Translate proved invaluable. I was encouraged in this endeavor by my children and siblings.

In April of 2018, I flew to Paris, took the train to Strasbourg, rented a car, and started my journey in Alsace. It was from there that my maternal great-grandparents had emigrated to the USA in the 1870s. Although my great-grandmother's maiden name was Wolfe—decidedly German rather than French—my great-grandfather did not want to be a German citizen. Their small town of Ashpach was reverting to German control after France had lost the most recent war with Germany. After seeing the local church and browsing in the attached cemetery, I drove across northern France through Reims and spent three weeks in Honfleur, a medieval city on the coast in Normandy.

The Saturday overnight in Reims, chosen because it was halfway across the country, proved to be serendipitous. The medieval cathedral there had been badly damaged during the First World War. The stained glass windows were replaced with magnificent new ones designed by French artist Marc Chagall. On Sunday morning I attended Mass said in French with Gregorian chant sung in Latin by an a capella quartet. I was able to follow enough of the sermon to understand the theme. Many of the prayers were familiar from my years in a Catholic girls' high school. The cathedral was dedicated to St. Remy—St. Remigius in English—who crowned and baptized the first king of France at that location in the sixth century. My birthday is October 1, which is listed in the church calendar as the feast of St. Remigius. Before this trip I knew that he was a bishop, but not much else.

While staying in Honfleur I drove to Bayeux to see the nearly one-thousand-year-old tapestry depicting the 1066 Battle of Hastings. I viewed the tapestry, visited the nearby cathedral, strolled around the picturesque town, had a snack in a local café, and started the return trip to where I had parked the car. I ended up at the Battle of Normandy Memorial Museum, not where I wanted to be. Here I was in a country not my own, where I was not fluent in the language, and lost. I had parked the car on the ring road and followed the directed footpath into the center of town. Somehow I managed to get on a similar path out of town that led me to a different destination. My cell phone battery had died. I didn't know what to do. All I could do was pray. "Dear Lord, please help me!" I stopped the first car I saw with people in it and said in my pitiful French, "Parlez-vous anglais?" An older man answered that yes, they were English, and did I need help? I guess the gray-haired lady with the cane didn't seem threatening to him and his adult son, his passenger. I explained the situation and asked if they could just drive me along the ring road. I was sure that I would recognize where I had left my car. That we did. The helpful man waited until I was in my car before he drove away.

This was a major lesson in trusting God: that my life is in God's hands and that God will guide me, if only I do trust that God will. The whole trip taught me that with God's help I could be self-sufficient and happy by myself. That experience gave me the courage to spend the next two years in seminary in New York City.

This was my second adventure as a widow, maybe even my third if I count moving from Boston to Onset, to the first home that was truly mine alone. April in France prepared me for other challenges, like going back to school at age seventy-two. I worried about keeping up with people less than half my age, with legs that ran marathons and ears that heard whispers. Turns out I *did* know Scripture, not like my professor, Dr. Julie Faith Parker, but as well as many in the class. And my memory wasn't so bad either. I remembered Katura and the Assyrians and Jesus's saying on the Sabbath faster than the twenty-somethings and the Ivy Leaguers and the preachers' kids that were my classmates. But best of all was when I went out on a limb to declare my faith in Teilhard de Chardin and Julian of Norwich and a gracious God who chuckles at our belief in doctrinal differences, to soothe the doubts and calm the fears of another student not looking for a decent grade, but seeking only the joy of participating in the divine midrash.

An important lesson in gratitude happened during my time at General Seminary. I found myself actually crying because I didn't know how to express my thanks for the intense and life-changing experience I was enjoying at GTS. I needed help. I sought advice from Heather Sisk, another older woman with whom I had become friends. When I explained my dilemma her answer was, "Use the gift."

At some point in my life I began to see education as security. It is one thing that can never be taken away. When in doubt, go back to school. This was subconscious for me until a therapist I was seeing at the time pointed it out to me. We were going through

Growing Through Grief

a rough patch where Bill's office was struggling and he wasn't drawing a paycheck. During that period I managed to convince the management of my firm to pay for a course in quality assurance given by a local biotech company. As I described this to the therapist she suddenly exclaimed, "Education is your security." My intelligence was the one thing I could always fall back on. The best way I had managed to protect this was by getting more formal education. Of course travel is education. Mark Twain wisely said, "Travel is fatal to prejudice, bigotry and narrow-mindedness."[1]

In reviewing these first years of widowhood, two themes stand out: education and travel. Travel has been a significant element in this journey. This doesn't sound particularly spiritual unless we look at it as pilgrimage. I think of pilgrimage as a contemplative journey to locations of spiritual significance for the purpose of self-examination. A worthwhile pilgrimage often results in personal transformation that lasts long after the actual journey. In describing the Celtic myth of the immram (sacred journey), Bernadette Flanagan and Michael O'Sullivan state,

> The mythological heroic figures leave the safe and familiar behind them in order to undertake great adventures into the utterly unknown. Fraught with challenges and gifts, perils and pleasures, these journeys offer the opportunity for transformation.[2]

In retrospect I see that this applies to all the traveling I did after Bill died. Perhaps it even applies to the experience of becoming a widow. Accepting and even embracing one's new identity is crucial to moving beyond grief. From my own experience as a widow, I can verify the centrality of dealing with identity. "Who am I now?" was an ever-present, nagging question. I took the journey through grief to a new identity literally. My whole month in France was a pilgrimage to learn who I was by myself, no longer in a professional and personal partnership. During that month I did visit two religious sites that had particular meaning for me. The church

---

1. Twain, *Innocents Abroad*, 650.
2. Flanagan and O'Sullivan, "Spirituality in Contemporary Ireland," 60.

Was I Unique?

calendar has listed two saints for October 1, my birthday. Traditionally it was St. Remigius, or Remy in France. More recently it is St. Therésè. I spent time at her basilica in Lisieux and at the cathedral in Reims where Remy was bishop.

I have long been drawn to T. S. Eliot's masterpiece *The Four Quartets*. His lines are even more poignant to me now. In particular, I resonate with the following from "Little Gidding," the final quartet:

> We shall not cease from exploration
> And the end of all our exploring
> Will be to arrive where we started
> And know the place for the first time.[3]

---

3. Eliot, *Four Quartets*, 35.

Chapter 2

Spirituality

ACCORDING TO THE OXFORD English Dictionary, spirituality is "the quality or condition of being spiritual; attachment to or regard for things of the spirit as opposed to material or worldly interests."[1]

Philip Sheldrake is an internationally recognized scholar who studied history, philosophy and theology at Oxford. Writing on the foundations of spirituality, he has said, "Modern spirituality centers on the deepest values and meanings by which people live."[2]

In her book *The Gifts of Imperfection*, Brené Brown defines spirituality as follows:

> Spirituality is recognizing and celebrating that we are all inextricably connected to each other by a power greater than all of us, and that our connection to that power and to one another is grounded in love and compassion. Practicing spirituality brings a sense of perspective, meaning, and purpose to our lives.[3]

Practicing spirituality can take various forms. For some people it can be attending services at church, temple, or mosque. For others, it's about nonreligious experiences such as reflection, time

---

1. Oxford English Dictionary, "spirituality."
2. Sheldrake, *Brief History of Spirituality*, 2.
3. Brown, *Gifts of Imperfection*, 86.

SPIRITUALITY

in nature, private prayer, yoga, or meditation. Another quote from Dr. Brown reiterates what my friend Rev. Heather Sisk advised me to do back in the Chapel of the Good Shepherd at General Seminary: "Use the gift."[4]

> Most of us who are searching for spiritual connection spend too much time looking up at the sky and wondering why God lives so far away. God lives within us, not above us. Sharing our gifts and talents with the world is the most powerful source of connection with God.[5]

Many people identify as spiritual but not religious. With a few exceptions, the percentage of adults who identify as religious in many industrialized countries is declining, while remaining generally high in less developed nations. "Even as religious affiliation decreases, though, a sense of spiritual identification could remain steady or even increase."[6]

An article in the *American Journal of Geriatric Psychiatry* concludes that "every individual has spirituality rooted in three core needs: the need to seek meaning and direction, the need to find self-worth and to belong to community, and the need to love and be loved, often facilitated through seeking reconciliation when relationships are broken."[7]

A similar explanation is given by Christopher Miller in his book *The Spiritual Artist: We Are Designed to Create*: "Sacred energy includes love, appreciation, awe, forgiveness, compassion, and acceptance."[8]

PERSONAL SPIRITUAL AUTOBIOGRAPHY

During my time studying in Ireland one assignment was to write a spiritual autobiography. This experience proved to be very

---

4. See chapter 1.
5. Brown, *Gifts of Imperfection*, 143.
6. Psychology Today, "Spirituality," para. 2.
7. Morgan et al., "Spiritual Care," abstract.
8. Miller, *Spiritual Artist*, 32.

powerful. I have lived a long life, even by biblical standards—more than the promised three score and ten. This exercise has shown me patterns and people in a new perspective. I have reviewed my childhood, early education through college, two marriages, two children, and now three grandchildren. I had a satisfying and rewarding career as an architectural specifications writer. As the General Thanksgiving in the *Common Prayer* says, "We thank you for setting us at tasks which demand our best efforts, and for leading us to accomplishments that satisfy and delight us."[9]

The four people that most influenced my spiritual journey were my grandmother, a college professor, my second husband, and my spiritual director of twenty-five years. I am the oldest of eight children. We grew up in my grandmother's house. My father worked for the airlines on an irregular schedule and was seldom home. My mother seemed always frazzled with crying babies, ubiquitous laundry, and meal preparation at odd hours. It was my grandmother who dominated the family. She set the rules and the tone. She and my father didn't speak to each other. My mother was the go-between for them.

It was this maternal grandmother from whom I learned to pray. She said the rosary every night on her knees, often kneeling at the side of my bed. I felt closer to her than to my parents. My father was often absent, my mother was stressed and frazzled with all the younger children. My grandmother would listen to us. She too was busy. She was a very talented seamstress, who made all her own clothes, my mother's wedding dress, and lots of beautiful clothes for her granddaughters. Somehow she was less stressed and more organized than my mother and was able to see each child as an individual.

Ours was a very religious Irish Catholic family.[10] My mother had a brother who was a priest, and my father had two sisters

---

9. Guilbert, *Book of Common Prayer*, 836.

10. I say Irish Catholic because this was a distinct version of Roman Catholicism practiced in Boston after World War II. Polish Catholics also lived in our neighborhood, but they had their own church and school where the services were said in Polish and the language was taught in the school.

Spirituality

who were nuns. No one would ever think of not going to Mass on Sunday. In May we always had an altar dedicated to the Blessed Mother. For each of us girls the dream was to crown the statue of Mary during the May procession when we were in eighth grade. None of us ever achieved this honor.

All eight of us were confirmed in our local parish and the oldest five were married in that same Most Precious Blood Church. The oldest six of us went to Catholic elementary school. Four of us went to Catholic high school, and I went to a Jesuit College. I had the most Catholic education, yet I was the first of us to turn my back on the church. Now three of my siblings are still practicing Catholics, three seldom go to church, one sister lives in Texas and attends a Protestant megachurch, and there is me, a dedicated Episcopalian.

I was a very pious child. I belonged to the Saint of the Month Book Club. Many of the saints had mottos. I decided that I needed one too. What I settled on was "God's will is my will." The difficulty with this is determining just what is God's will. Only recently have I learned about Ignatian spirituality and the use of consolation and desolation as guides in decision-making.

I was hyper responsible to my parents and for my younger siblings. This was encouraged, and even mandated, by my parents and grandmother. When I was eight years old it was my job to take my baby brother out in his carriage for an hour every day. My father repeatedly told me that it was my responsibility to get a scholarship to college and then put my younger brothers and sisters through also. I took this very seriously. I did win a four-year scholarship to Boston College and after graduation paid my brother's tuition to a Jesuit high school. Some of that was during the time I was a VISTA volunteer earning fifty dollars a week. That program provided for some money to be put away for us to receive after our volunteer time was complete. It was that money I arranged to have sent to my brother's school.

Another example of taking on the responsibility that rightfully belonged to my parents was when one of my younger sisters was continually complaining about excruciating pain in her ear.

Growing Through Grief

My mother kept dismissing this so I arranged for an appointment at Massachusetts Eye and Ear Infirmary. I was probably in college at this time, still living at home. My sister Marie was probably about six years old. The ear, nose, and throat specialist determined that Marie had a perforated ear drum. No wonder she was in so much pain, especially when she was in the water! At this point my parents did take over and saw Marie through the required surgery.

During high school my first real boyfriend broke my heart by leaving me for a close friend of mine that he met while she was staying at my house. I found solace by throwing myself into work on a science project. In retrospect I'm really glad I didn't marry him. He and his wife had thirteen children. Looking back, I see God protecting me. I had broken trust with the boyfriend by sharing his recent diabetes diagnosis with my uncle, a medical professional. The boyfriend wanted sex as atonement for my betrayal. I couldn't or wouldn't do that.

Around this time I won a full scholarship to Boston College. Said boyfriend was threatened by the scholarship. He knew that I had applied and said he didn't want to know the outcome. I didn't tell him. His future wife didn't go to college. They married when he graduated. She was nineteen.

Like all Catholic girls who attended girls' schools taught by nuns, I was being groomed to enter the convent after graduation. I saw the opportunity to go to college as God telling me this was my next strep. It confirmed my decision not to enter the convent at this time. In retrospect this was my first example of Ignatian consolation. It was also not the last time a man was threatened by my intelligence.

About ten years later my then husband dissuaded me from going to law school because he feared I would be a better lawyer than he was. He did, however, point me in the direction of my lifelong career. He said, "Why don't you go to architecture school? You're always looking at buildings." So I did and loved it. For thirty years my professional work was in architecture. I was a specifications writer, putting into words those aspects of the construction process that could not be shown in drawings. I documented

SPIRITUALITY

materials, procedures, quality control, sequence of events, and applicable governmental regulations.

That man saw me as Little Lulu, a cartoon character who was always there with a box of tissues. I am an Enneagram 2, the Helper. Did he know me better than I knew myself? He was also the first man I looked to for representing what I saw as admirable traits that I lacked but aspired to. He was a rebel; I was Goody Two-Shoes. He represented adventure, stepping outside the box, going against what was expected. As a second-wave feminist I am embarrassed by how much I looked to men to define me. The funny thing is that each time I did this I ended up being able to acquire those characteristics for myself.

This first marriage ended after seven years in a very messy divorce. It was too easy to blame my husband for leaving me for his secretary, who was younger, blonder, and thinner than I. Upon reflection I learned that I was not without fault. Picking up the pieces and getting back on an even keel took time and a lot of hard work. I learned that God works in mysterious ways and that God can redeem any situation. It took ten years for me to forgive them and even longer to forgive myself. Because of that experience I am stronger, more self-reliant, and more appreciative of truly loving relationships.

That marriage also gave me my beloved daughter and now my darling granddaughter. Over the ensuing years I worked hard to maintain the relationship between my daughter and her father. At times it was very difficult, but I knew it was important for all three of us.

TURNING POINT

Mary Daly was a pioneering second-wave feminist thinker. She was my teacher at Boston College for two semesters. In her first book, *The Church and the Second Sex*, she documented the misogyny of the Roman Catholic Church over the centuries. She seemed particularly angry about the refusal of the church to ordain women to the priesthood. Her next book was *Beyond God the Father: The*

Sisterhood of Cosmic Consciousness. She went on to write several more books, each one more radically feminist and less concerned with Christianity and traditional deity.

While her student, I complained to Dr. Daly that she had taken away my faith and given me nothing in return. She answered, "There is nothing." I have ruminated and reflected on that statement over the years. At one point I thought, "What if I see that as No Thing? Is that God?" Was I to replace the empty rituals of a restrictive tradition with a recognition and relationship with a Being unlike any other?

Through Mary Daly's classes I was also introduced to Paul Tillich and Pierre Teilhard de Chardin. Tillich's Ground of Being and Teilhard's Alpha and Omega points became my first non-traditional concepts of God.[11] Those ideas continue to resonate for me. My father once said that I went to college and lost my faith. That is probably true. The faith I lost was an immature one, with a punishing God and the necessity to earn *his* love. In the following years, actually the rest of my life, that immature faith has been replaced by a personal God in whom I live and move and have my being. I have learned that I am a panentheist. I believe that God is everywhere and in every thing, truly the ground of being, the élan vital of Henri Bergson. As my favorite psalm, 139, says,

> Where can I go from your spirit?
> Or where can I flee from your presence?
>   If I climb up to heaven, you are there;
> if I make the grave my bed, you are there also.
>   If I take the wings of the morning
> and dwell in the uttermost parts of the sea,
>   Even there your hand shall lead me,
> your right hand hold me fast.[12]

It wasn't just feminism that drove me from the church. This was the 1960s. War was raging in Vietnam. Our friends were being drafted right out of graduate school. My first husband and I had

---

11. Tillich, *Systematic Theology*, 84–287; Teilhard de Chardin, *Human Phenomenon*, 183.

12. Guilbert, *Book of Common Prayer*, 794.

been married in the church and our daughter had been baptized as a Roman Catholic. Now we saw the church as hypocritical in its stance on the war. We marched on Washington in protest. I saw (and still see) the term *just war* as a contradiction in terms. For me, war must only be the very last resort after all other means of conflict resolution have been exhausted. We didn't just *fall away* from the church. We left in the anger of our young idealism.

RETURN TO FAITH

I first met Bill Buckingham when I was a student at the Boston Architectural College and he was on the faculty. I never took one of his classes, but somehow I had formed a negative impression of him. I saw him as pompous and arrogant, always pontificating about some building or theory. After I graduated with my bachelor of architecture degree, I had an interview with one of the downtown Boston architectural firms. When I arrived, I saw the names of the partners listed on the entrance door. I was surprised to see William Buckingham was among them. I almost turned around to leave, but knew I wanted that job.

I was hired as a graphic designer in the twenty-five-person firm. Over the following months I got to know Bill as well as the other people in the office. One of the things that struck me about him was that he never engaged in gossip. We often had lunch together. For some reason I mentioned that I wanted to go to a fundraiser dance that was being held at my daughter's school. It was formal and I didn't have an escort. Bill said, "I own my own tuxedo. It was required at my college." He volunteered to be my escort. That became our first date.

Shortly after this Bill invited me to a concert at his church. We ended up attending the Maundy Thursday Eucharist that year. It had been years since I had gone to church, but I gladly went in order to spend more time with him. My reaction was, "This is the church of my childhood!" It was a high Anglican Episcopal church. The vestments, furnishings and liturgy reminded me of the Roman Catholic church I had grown up in, before all the changes brought about by Vatican II. It all seemed very familiar and filled a void in my life. Bill and church continued to be intertwined. I knew that he went to 7:00 a.m. Mass every weekday so I started doing that occasionally. I remember saying to the priest, "Am I coming to attend Mass or for a chance to spend time with Bill?" He responded that it wasn't my motivation that mattered, but just the fact of my presence. I guess that is what is meant by the saying "Ninety percent of success is just showing up."[13]

At some point during this courtship I decided that I needed to go to confession. It seemed like an appropriate ritual to mark my return to religious practice. I wanted God's forgiveness for all I had done during the lean years when I wasn't actively expressing my faith. The wise priest said, "Margery, God forgives you; you have to forgive yourself."

Acceptance was something I had long struggled with. I remember telling Bill at some point that I had cut off parts of myself—the wild and unconventional parts—to fit an image of what I thought he wanted. His gracious response was, "But, Margery, it's you I married." How could I not love this man who gave me back my faith? The marriage was often difficult for me, but I never regretted loving him.

GROWING IN FAITH

Eunice Schatz was my spiritual director for twenty-five years. Our relationship began when she was a career counselor and I was exploring options. Over the years she became a spiritual director through the Shalem program. She was the only person in my life with whom I was completely honest. It was through her that I was introduced to the Enneagram. I am a 2, the Helper. When that was first identified, I hated the idea. I wanted to be a Four—unique and artistic. Interestingly, Four is the direction to which the evolved Two heads.

---

13. Attributed to Woody Allen. See "Quote Origin."

SPIRITUALITY

Eunice was a Jungian. Together we did a lot of dream work. She didn't always approve of choices I made, but she was always supportive and encouraging. She was a role model and mentor for me, especially in my exploration of becoming a spiritual director myself. In 2018 she suffered a stroke and had to stop working. In seminary in New York and in my Irish master's program the schools paid for us to meet with a spiritual director that we chose from an approved list. I still meet with my Irish director, usually on Zoom unless I am in Ireland, when we meet in person.

After I returned to church in the 1980s I learned that my spiritual life thrived best in small groups. First it was a women's group at All Saints Ashmont, Bill's Anglo-Catholic parish. We met during the day, read scripturally based books, and sang praise music. In Philadelphia it was house church that met twice a month in the evening at the members' houses. We read and discussed spiritual books, had dessert and coffee, and ended with Compline. In Princeton, a similar group was called a covenant group. The format was similar, but instead of a book we discussed a topic presented by that session's host. In each of these groups I formed long-lasting friendships as my faith deepened. I learned that my spiritual life grows best in the company of other like-minded souls and within the framework and discipline of an organized program.

Most recently I have been involved in a Thursday morning Eucharist and Bible study that has been meeting for over thirty years. The members change and the leadership changes, but the format remains the same. We begin at ten o'clock with an informal Eucharist celebrated on a coffee table with about a dozen participants gathered around on sofas and comfortable chairs. The sermon is usually a discussion by all present on the day's readings. We often use the propers for the upcoming Sunday. After the Eucharist we have coffee and pastry before a lively commentary on whichever book of the Bible we are studying. I have belonged to this group for over fifteen years. In the last few years I have been invited to lead both the sermon discussion and the Bible presentation. I find this a joy and a privilege and always look forward to my turn. During COVID, we began to meet on Zoom. Since moving away from Boston I have continued with virtual attendance except when I am leading. Then I drive the fifty miles to St. Michael's church in Milton.

While my husband was alive I was content to live in his spiritual shadow. He was a pillar of his high Anglo-Catholic parish in Boston. He continued to have the familiar zeal of a convert. Bill was brought up in the Church of Christ in Great Falls, Montana. He discovered the Episcopal Church when he was a student in Cambridge, Massachusetts. The music, ritual, and tradition were much more aligned with his formal approach to life than the fundamentalist church of his childhood, which didn't have a presence in New England.

TRANSITION

In the 1990s I went on a five-day silent retreat at a facility run by the Anglican monastic order called the Society of St. John the Evangelist. It took me over a year to arrange my work and family life to be able to do this. I thought I was going on this retreat to decide the future of my marriage. This was during the beginning of my emotional involvement with a man I had met at church. We talked on the phone every day. Before I left for the retreat we had a serious argument that led me to believe that the relationship was over. My conclusion was that this was not to be the focus of the retreat.

Early in the week of the retreat I had an experience that was very new to me. I wasn't really sure what to call it. This was the first time it happened, but it was not the last. I *heard* the phrase, "To have nothing but you, Oh Lord, is to have everything." I've learned that this is called interior locution. St. Teresa of Avila, the sixteenth-century Spanish Carmelite, goes into great detail about interior locution in her masterpiece *The Interior Castle*.[14] She explains how to recognize, affirm, and respond to this phenomenon when it occurs.

---

14. Smith, *Interior Castle*, 152.

Spirituality

The second time this happened was when I was attending a Friday morning Eucharist during my eighteen-month period of living in Princeton, New Jersey. This time what I heard was, "All that I am is of you, O Lord." The parts of myself that I don't like, my character flaws, my failures, my inadequacies are all acceptable to God. This is difficult for me to accept.

The personal failing that gives me the most trouble is my tendency to say what is on my mind without considering the consequences. Sometimes I just blurt things out without thinking. Because of this I have hurt people without even realizing it. Much later they tell me what I have done and I am deeply sorry. One of my sisters says that I don't have a filter. In discussing this with my spiritual director I was able to identify that the cause of this is often a desire to impress people with my wit. The Enneagram tells me that the sin of the 2 is pride. Perhaps this is one example of how pride manifests itself in me.

A third instance of interior locution occurred during an informal Eucharist when the priest extended her hand to touch the elements while saying, "This is my body." It was instantly clear to me that she could have touched the table, the wall, the candles, or anything else and the words would still be true. This is the panentheism that I mentioned earlier in reference to Paul Tillich and the concept of God as the Ground of Being. In addition to God being in everything, panentheism believes that everything is in God.

Recently I was thinking about these messages and decided I wanted another one. I prayed about it and received the words, "You have enough." Like the first three messages, this one is not simple. What did I have enough of? Enough messages, enough stuff in my life, enough grace to carry out God's plan for me? I wasn't sure. But like the earlier messages, this one gave me plenty to contemplate. Maybe I heard incorrectly; maybe it was, "You are enough." Again it raises questions—enough for what?

Since retiring from my work as an architectural specifications writer, I have learned that I no longer need to strive for success, whether that is career achievement or even spiritual success, however that might be defined. It is very similar to letting go of the need to earn God's love. St. Therese of Lisieux is quoted as saying, "All that is necessary is surrender and gratitude."

Surrender has been difficult for me. It is like the twelve-step saying "Let go and let God." It took me years to understand the meaning of that phrase. Only when someone explained that it meant "Let go of the outcome" did it begin to make sense to me. For example, if a homeless person asks for money, it is not my responsibility to determine if they are going to buy cigarettes or drugs. Scripture is very clear on this. I now believe my obligation is to do the right thing, for the right reason, and not worry about the results.

Angeles Arrien, writing in her book *The Second Half of Life*, delves deeper into the idea that nonattachment to outcome is central to real satisfaction and acceptance:

> Nothing suffocates the life force more thoroughly than trying to control what is happening. Rather than trying to assert control over relationships, health, work, or any other aspect of life where we do not trust, we need to know that in the situations that are important to us, we have planned and prepared well. Then we can be open to possibilities and outcomes that we may not have considered.[15]

---

15. Arrien, *Second Half of Life*, 140.

Chapter 3

Widowhood

WIDOWHOOD IS A CLUB no one wants to belong to and no one wants to join. Despite that, historically speaking, this is probably the best time to be a widow, particularly in Western culture.

In the patriarchal world of the Bible, women usually could not inherit the wealth of their fathers or husbands. If a woman bore no son and her husband died, she could fall into abject poverty. Among the last and the least in their society, widows were often in the fields at harvest time, to gather in the last and the least of the produce.[1]

ORDER OF WIDOWS

One of the ways the early Christian church addressed this problem was by the establishment of the Order of Widows.

> The true innovation in early Christian communities was not in coming to the aid of the widows, which had been long considered a meritorious act by the Israelites. Nor was it in simply acknowledging them as members of the community. Rather, it was in discovering genuine ways

---

1. Parkerton, *Where You Go*, xv.

in which the widows could aid others, thereby creating an innovative form of social unity.[2]

In a 2006 article, M. Cathleen Kaveny, then professor of law and professor of theology at the University of Notre Dame, noted that through an order of widows, the early church "recognized the contribution that the widows could make to the well-being and spiritual growth of their fellow believers."[3]

Together with identity, isolation stands out as a difficult challenge for older widows. As Kaveny explains, this is not a new problem. What *is* new is the greater number of widows in society today as all people live longer and more women outlive men. Kaveny is suggesting that encouraging community and purpose for widows will help alleviate these problems.

"The Order of Widows can trace its biblical roots to 1 Timothy, where its qualifications for membership are listed alongside the qualifications for the ecclesiastical offices of bishop, deacon, and elder," Kaveny wrote. "These qualifications include age (a widow must be 60 years old), only one marriage (widows must remain continent after their husbands die), and a history of good deeds."[4] Kaveny said that the primary duty of the Order of Widows was to pray ceaselessly on behalf of the community.

> Their pleas are powerful because God hears the cries of the oppressed. Although theirs was not a ministry of the altar, they exercised spiritual authority and influence in their ministry to the community. Widows made house visitations, where they comforted, fasted, and prayed with the sick and gave practical instruction to younger women. They prophesied. Enrolled widows also assumed a place of honor in the liturgy, sitting in the front of the assembly along with the bishops, priests, and deacons.[5]

---

2. Kaveny, "Order of Widows," 18.
3. Kaveny, "Order of Widows," 16.
4. Kaveny, "Order of Widows," 16.
5. Kaveny, "Order of Widows," 16.

There were orders of widows in the early church, up until the Middle Ages. At that time the legal status of widows changed for the better. "The medieval widow was a visible figure in society, a part of the public working sphere and the private domestic sphere, partaking in most of the male dominated spaces, which could have been threatening to male-ordered society, and possibly the reason for the new set of challenges placed against all females in the sixteenth century."[6]

There is currently renewed interest in the Order of Widows. On October 16, 2024, Bishop Earl Fernandes of the Diocese of Columbus, Ohio, issued a decree to establish the *Ordo Viduarum*, or the Order of Widows, as a community of diocesan right. It is open to widows over sixty who have been sacramentally married. The initial response was six women.

LESBIAN WIDOWS

Vicky Whipple is the author of a book subtitled *Invisible Grief*. She herself is a lesbian widow. In the book, she documents her own experience and that of twenty-four additional lesbian widows. The book was published in 2006, before legal marriage for gay and lesbian couples was enacted in the United States. Whipple states,

> In addition to the difference in the very nature of the relationship of two women and the emotional investment women make in their relationships, heterosexism and homophobia act as catalysts to draw lesbian partners even closer together as a defense against the world's hostility. Heterosexism, the belief that everyone is and must be heterosexual, results in lesbian relationships being invisible and unrecognized in the world at large. Lesbian couples must create a home life and a support network that counteract these negative messages from society. This further reinforces the already close nature of lesbian relationships.[7]

---

6. Jerrard, "Traditionally Widowhood Has Been."
7. Whipple, *Lesbian Widows: Invisible Grief*, 6.

A situation where a partner experiences a loss that is not openly acknowledged is called disenfranchised grief. This will be discussed further in chapter 4, "Grief."

At the most painful time in their lives, many lesbians are treated as if they do not exist, have faced having their relationship ignored or minimized, or have felt forced to come out to obtain help. One caretaker was denied family leave. Widows who have lost husbands do not face these issues. Their relationships and their grief are publicly recognized and honored. It is interesting to note that the majority of the widows in Whipple's book were out and experienced no discrimination. It was primarily those who were not out who encountered problems. However, the fact that so many lesbians were out and received support, Whipple believes, reflects the historical time in which these events happened. Such openness would not have been possible twenty, thirty, forty years ago.[8]

The following paragraph from *Lesbian Widows* applies to all bereaved people who have lost a significant other:

> One of the myths that people tend to believe about grief is that the goal should be to get over your grief as soon as possible. Friends may tell us we should pack away her pictures or keep busy to avoid thinking about her. But the truth is that we will never get over our loss and we will never forget someone we have loved that deeply. What we do is learn to live with our grief. We change our relationship with our deceased partner to one of memory rather than one of having her physically present with us.[9]

THEN AND NOW

Three women writers—two widows and one married priest—collaborated on a book subtitled *Gleanings from the Stories of Biblical*

---

8. Whipple, *Lesbian Widows: Invisible Grief*, 67.
9. Whipple, *Lesbian Widows: Invisible Grief*, 161.

Widows.[10] They tell the stories of eight widows, six from the Hebrew Scriptures[11] and two from the New Testament.[12] After each of these, the two widowed authors relate a piece of their own bereavement that relates to that chapter. There are similarities and differences in the authors' lives since Jane's husband dropped dead while out running and Anne's husband suffered through a year of cancer. Jane had three young children while Anne had grown stepchildren, but none of her own. All three authors were members of the same church in Brooklyn and had been friends before the events in the book.

> As much as for the widows of the Bible, social alienation besets widows today. Afraid of the too-close reality of death, people, even close friends, often subtly shun widows just when we most need companionship. People seem uncomfortable hearing about our grief, about how our husbands or partners died, about how difficult it is for us to be single again, or even about the funny, joyful stories of our past loves.[13]

DECISIONS, DECISIONS

A small, but not insignificant, decision widows need to make is whether or not to continue to wear their wedding ring. Some leave it right where their spouse placed it however many years ago. Some wear it on a gold or silver chain around their neck. I don't wear mine. My daughter asked me why, and I responded, "I'm not married anymore." But my ring finger still bears the mark left by that ring. A similar decision is how we choose to be formally

---

10. Parkerton, *Where You Go*.

11. Abigail (1 Sam 25:2–42), Naomi (Ruth 1:1–22) Tamar (Gen 38:1–26) Judith (Jdt 8:1—16:25), Ruth (the book of Ruth) and the widow of Zarephath (1 Kgs 17:8–24).

12. Anna (Luke 2:36–38) and the widow with two coins (Mark 12:38–44 and Luke 21:1–4).

13. Parkerton, *Where You Go*, xvii.

addressed. Etiquette says I am now Mrs. Margery Buckingham, not Mrs. William Buckingham. Some widows prefer Ms.

The only way to stop being a widow is to remarry. This may be a compelling option for younger women, especially those with young children. Research shows that widowed men are more likely to remarry than widowed women. When I asked my interviewees about this topic, for various reasons none of them were eager to remarry. Nonnie is sixty years old. She explained, "If I ever found someone, they're going to be in their sixties, at least, and I don't want to go through that again. I don't want to get so close to somebody that I'm going to have to take care of them and they're going to die on me again. So right now I say, 'No.'"[14] Abigail says, "I could never find another person like him. He was unique. No one could ever replace him."[15] Some candidly admit that they miss sex, but for many widows it is the loneliness that bothers them more. Karen said, "I might enjoy an affair, but I've grown accustomed to living alone and I like it. I don't want to accommodate another person in my home."[16] I've been known to say something similar: "I'd like a man in my life, but not in my house." Anne has been widowed for nineteen years and didn't mention dating or remarriage. She has lots of friends and family and isn't lonely.[17] Patricia might like the companionship but isn't interested in dating after being away from it for fifty years.[18]

In her book *Surviving Grief*, Catherine Sanders talks about remarriage, but cautions that it can lead to disappointment if the

---

14. Interview with the author, Apr. 26, 2022. Subsequent quotations from Nonnie are also from this interview.

15. Interview with the author, May 17, 2022. Subsequent quotations from Abigail are also from this interview.

16. Interview with the author, Apr. 28, 2022. Subsequent quotations from Karen are also from this interview.

17. Interview with the author, Apr. 25, 2022. Subsequent quotations from Anne are also from this interview.

18. Interview with the author, May 4, 2022. Subsequent quotations from Patricia are also from this interview.

woman has not allowed enough time to be comfortable with her new identity.[19]

One of the more consequential decisions we face is whether or not to move from our marital home. Sometimes there is pressure from our adult children to live with or move closer to them. That could mean moving to a different state and leaving behind existing support systems and familiar surroundings. We don't want to rush into a decision that we may regret later and not have the option to reverse. Conventional wisdom suggests that we not make any big decisions during the first year of our bereavement.

With the support of family and friends and the grace of God, we can survive, but we must remember that it takes time, it won't be easy, and some days will be harder than others. If we summon our inner strength, seek out role models, and exercise creativity, we will not only survive, but grow through our grief.

---

19. Sanders, *Surviving Grief*, 153–54.

Chapter 4

Grief

ALTHOUGH OFTEN USED INTERCHANGEABLY, grief refers to the emotion following a loss, while mourning is the process of expressing and working through that grief. In other words, grief is internal and mourning is external.

> *Grief* refers to the emotions, thoughts, and behaviors that a person experiences after a significant loss, such as the death of a loved one, the end of a relationship, or a major life change. Grief is a natural and normal response to loss, and it can involve feelings of sadness, anger, guilt, or numbness. It may also involve physical symptoms such as fatigue, difficulty sleeping, or changes in appetite.
>
> *Mourning* is an expression of grief that involves adapting to the loss and integrating it into one's life. It is a more active process than grief and can involve a variety of rituals, customs, and behaviors that help individuals come to terms with their loss. Mourning might include activities such as funerals, memorial services, or personal rituals like creating a memory book or writing letters to the deceased.[1]

1. Lupcho, "Grief Vs. Mourning."

In 1969 Elisabeth Kubler-Ross wrote the blockbuster classic *On Death and Dying*, where she first defined the five stages of grief as denial, anger, bargaining, depression, and acceptance. Since then others have refined her work and modified the list of stages. Her collaborator, David Kessler, has proposed a sixth stage: meaning. His book *Finding Meaning: The Sixth Stage of Grief* interweaves his philosophy, his professional experience working with bereavement groups, and the process he went through after the death of his own adopted son at age twenty-one. Kessler invites his readers to find meaning in both the life of the lost loved one and in the life going forward for the bereaved.

Kessler equates meaning with growth and lists five specific ways people can grow after a tragedy such as bereavement:

1. Their relationships grow stronger.
2. They discover new purposes in life.
3. The trauma allows them to find their inner strength.
4. Their spirituality is deepened.
5. They renew their appreciation for life.[2]

John Monbourquette takes a different route to arrive at a similar destination. He describes eight stages of grief: shock, denial, expressing emotions and feelings, completing the tasks related to grieving, discovering the meaning of the loss, forgiveness, claiming the legacy, and celebrating the end of grief.[3] In your own way, you are also experiencing a form of death in yourself. For that reason, creating life around you is important.

Another book comprises a series of forty-six short chapters and three appendices by a layman committed to the Roman Catholic Church. Bill Dodds, the author, has written over three dozen books with his late wife, Monica. Together they founded the Friends of St. John the Caregiver, an international organization that promotes support for family caregivers.

---

2. Kessler, *Finding Meaning*, 158.
3. Monbourquette, *How to Love Again*, 48.

One comment Dodds makes that relates directly to spiritual development is the following: "With the passing of time and grace of God, sometimes it's possible to see that the deepest blessings have their roots in the hardest challenges."[4]

In chapter 36, "A Third Wheel: Your New Life in the Margin," Dodd discusses how widows and widowers can become socially unacceptable. He gives several possible reasons that the bereaved are left out of social gatherings. One was that wives saw widows as potential threats to their own marriages. A second was that the newly single person reminded the couples how fragile life was, that they could easily be in the same situation. A third possibility was that people didn't know what to say or how to act with the widow or widower. Dodds's advice in these situations is for the often excluded person to take the initiative, not to hold a formal dinner party, but maybe invite one person to meet for coffee or lunch. Word might get around that you aren't that scary after all.[5]

I personally appreciated and agreed with one of the pieces of advice Dodds lists in appendix 3, "A Handout Sheet to Share with Family and Friends."[6] He talks about how even the happiest moments can be tinged with sadness. Our son's wedding took place nine months after my husband died. Of course I was very happy for David and his bride, but I felt very alone and wished so much that Bill was there physically, even though I was assured by others that he was there in spirit.

MEANING AND BEREAVEMENT

In the literature of grief and loss, *meaning* is often cited as essential to the process of recovery after bereavement. David Kessler extends the five stages of grief beyond Elisabeth Kubler-Ross's original list of denial, anger, bargaining, depression, and acceptance to include a sixth stage, meaning. Kessler invites his readers to find

---

4. Dodds, *On Your Pilgrimage*, 121.
5. Dodds, *On Your Pilgrimage*, 100.
6. Dodds, *On Your Pilgrimage*, 138.

meaning in both the life of the lost loved one and in the life going forward for the bereaved.[7]

Robert A. Neimeyer, a leading academic researcher on grief, defines grieving as "a process of reconstructing a world of meaning that has been challenged by loss."[8] He further states that "meaning reconstruction is the central process in what we conventionally refer to as grieving."[9]

> Human beings are viewed as co-authors of their own life stories, struggling to compose a meaningful account of the important events of their lives and revising, editing, or even dramatically rewriting these when the presuppositions that sustain these accounts are challenged by unanticipated or incongruous events.[10]

Another article concludes by noting that a change is taking place in academic grief research:

> Now we are seeing a shift away from a sole emphasis on grief's devastation toward a realization that grief's consequences are not necessarily all bad and an awareness, perhaps reluctantly arrived at, that the quality of some people's lives is in some ways better following their loved one's death than it was before.[11]

Dr. James Hollis, a Jungian psychoanalyst, has the following insight:

> Suffering is spiritual, for inevitably it raises questions of meaning. If we are free of suffering, we are less likely to engage with those questions that ultimately define who we are. The rigor and depth of questions raised by suffering jar us out of complacency, out of causal reiterations

---

7. Kessler, *Finding Meaning*.
8. Neimeyer, "Language of Loss," 263.
9. Neimeyer, "Language of Loss," xii.
10. Neimeyer, "Language of Loss," 263.
11. Frantz et al., "Positive Outcomes of Losing," 206.

of untroubled life, and bring us to the daily dilemma of enlargement or diminishment.[12]

Hollis also says, "The only way to avoid loss is to avoid attachment, but to live without commitment is to live in an arid place."[13]

An article in *Nursing Forum* titled "Post-Traumatic Growth in Women Who Have Experienced the Loss of Their Spouse or Partner" mentions spiritual growth after widowhood, but it doesn't elaborate on what that means or how it happens. Fifteen women were interviewed. The article reports, "Six themes emerged from the data analysis: (1) Listen to my story of loss, (2) Pushing through the sadness, (3) Anticipated versus unanticipated loss, (4) A new depth of compassion and empathy, (5) My strength grew over time, and (6) My view of myself changed."[14]

As support of theme 6—"My view of myself changed"— Doherty explains that the widows "carefully reflected on their journey and recognized personal growth and strength, appreciation of life, a desire to help others, increased compassion and empathy, new possibilities, and a sense of spirituality."[15] The author comments, "When a person finds their way through trauma, they teach others about healing, coping, empathy, compassion, and the power of being connected to other human beings."[16]

Vicky Whipple is very explicit about what grief involves:

> In the months after we were widowed, we experienced a range of emotions including disorientation, sadness, anger, relief, guilt, loneliness, and longing. Grief work involves allowing ourselves to feel those feelings, no matter how painful they are, rather than denying or running away from them or drowning them with alcohol or drugs. This does not happen quickly or easily. One way to

---

12. Hollis, *Finding Meaning*, 210.
13. Hollis, *Finding Meaning*, 215.
14. Doherty and Scannell-Desch, "Post-Traumatic Growth," 78.
15. Doherty and Scannell-Desch, "Post-Traumatic Growth," 84.
16. Doherty and Scannell-Desch, "Post-Traumatic Growth," 85.

think of it is to understand that grief is not an event that happens but a process that we go through over time.[17]

ANTICIPATORY GRIEF

People expecting a loss may also experience anticipatory or preparatory grief. Rather than grieving for the person who is still alive, one may feel grief for things that won't happen in the future. My husband's diagnosis of terminal pulmonary fibrosis with a three- to five-year prognosis was more shocking to me than his actual death. He wasn't yet seventy years old. Gone were the dreams of leisurely travel and watching our grandchildren grow up.

My father died in January of 1997 of metastasized prostate cancer that had reached his bones. He had been in and out of the hospital for several months. One Sunday in church I started crying and couldn't stop. I had to leave my pew and go to the back of the sanctuary so that I didn't disturb the other worshipers. I had been a member for several years and it was a rather small and close knit congregation. The senior warden and his wife were ushering that day. They sat with me, listened to my story, and offered comfort as best they could until I regained my composure sufficiently to return to my seat. Two weeks later my father died. They and many others from that church attended the wake, which was in another town. Only later did I put a name, anticipatory grief, to what I had experienced.

DISENFRANCHISED GRIEF

Professionals use the term disenfranchised grief to describe a situation where a partner experiences a loss that is not openly acknowledged. This can be true for couples that are cohabiting, gay couples, and lesbian couples. Even though same-sex marriage is currently legal in the United States, for various reasons not all couples are public about their relationships.

17. Whipple, *Lesbian Widows: Invisible Grief*, 98.

Vicky Whipple says that she and her partner "experienced the pain of not having our loss acknowledged as the loss of a spouse until we made the decision to come out. Only then did we feel validated instead of invisible. Other lesbian widows, unable to come out for fear of losing their jobs, remained invisible."[18]

VISUALIZING GRIEF RESOLUTION

Because I am a visual person,[19] I like to see process depicted graphically. I developed an image that I felt represented my experience during bereavement and tested it along with two more alternatives. By far the new image, C, resonated with more people than A and B, the more conventional ones. For me this represents three steps forward and one step back during a continued positive resolution. In my own experience I can recognize and label occasions when I regressed and had to repeat my forward movement. Of course, I realize that we can't actually go back in time, but it certainly feels that way.

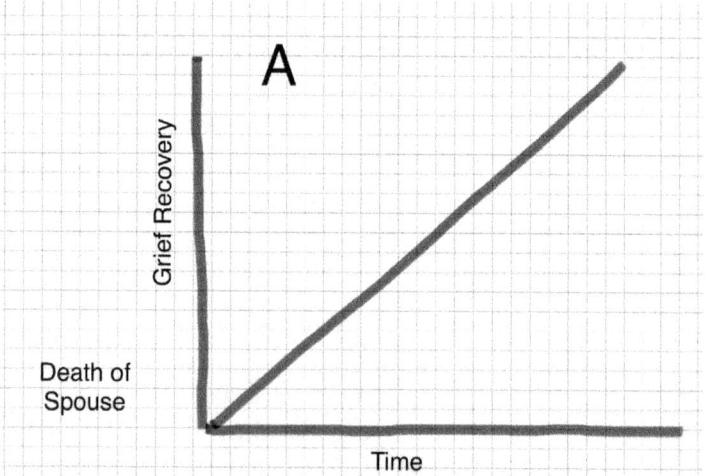

18. Whipple, *Lesbian Widows: Invisible Grief*, 109.
19. I have a degree in architecture and worked in that profession for thirty years.

GRIEF

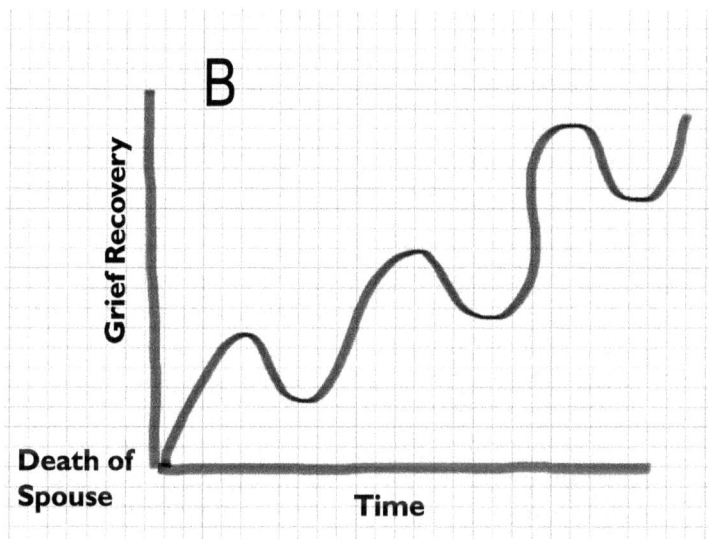

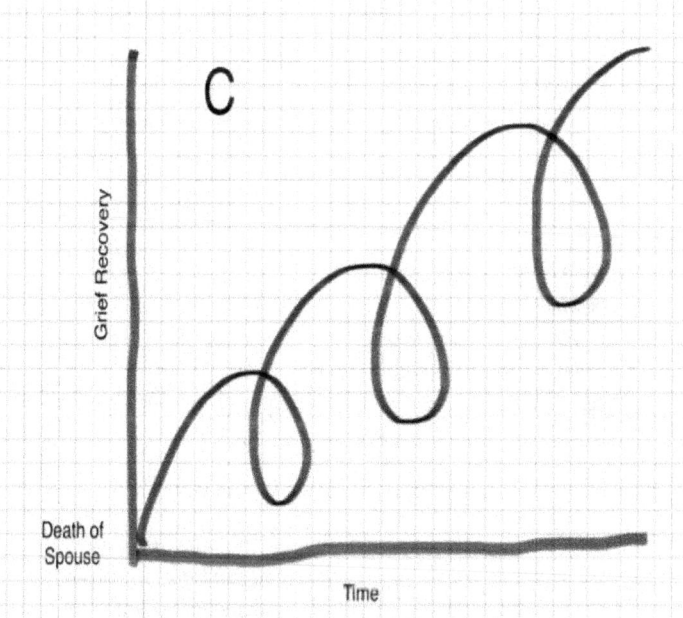

The following four women, who are identified by changed first names only, are the ones I interviewed for my Irish dissertation. You will hear more details of their stories in chapter 6, "The Widows Speak."

When I asked Nonnie if any of the three images above resonated with her, she replied,

> The third one (C), where you go up, and then you go down, and then up and down and up and down—the spirally one, the loopy one. That looked to me like you were doing pretty good. And then you went to the bottom again. And then you started to come up and rise again, and then you went to the bottom again.
>
> That feels like me because everybody said all of the firsts are going to be the worst. Well, you know what? The first year was difficult, all of the first holidays and everything. They were horrible. But I found the second year to be even worse.

Abigail, the Episcopal priest, selected the more conventional model, B, but like me, she was able without prompting to describe exactly when the first downward transition occurred.

Anne, the author and faculty member, also chose image C.

> The thing that makes that one even more helpful than the middle one is the fact that it loops backward multiple times.
>
> And so in other words, it isn't like, okay, there's some ups and downs, but it's all going like one direction. I love the loops. That's what makes this work. You're going forward, now you're going down, and now you're going back a little bit. That's exactly what grief looks like. That's brilliant!

Patricia explained her choice of image C this way:

> And then the spirally one is kind of the same to me, only that seems like less predictable that you're going up a little bit, but then you're sliding down, whereas with the squiggly line, you're continually going up, getting accustomed to this or dealing with it more successfully. And I

feel like the squiggly line is more what I'm feeling. Some days, I think, "you're okay." And then something reminds me of him and I slip back a little and feel like I have to start my recovery over again. And yet it's constantly evolving. Yes, in the right direction. And it's not linear. I feel like it's not a linear progression.

Mary Pipher also describes grief as a circular staircase:

> We feel better then we feel worse. Holidays, anniversaries, and many other things trigger grief reactions. We may have a rather good Year Two, and then be felled by Year Three. With intention and skills, we move forward on our journey, but not without spiraling in the waters.[20]

Vicky Whipple uses the idea of recycling when talking about resolving grief:

> Grief work is not a straight line. It has ups and downs, backs and forths, twists and turns. Just when we think we are finished grieving, we find ourselves grieving once again.[21]

The tenth anniversary of my husband's death was especially difficult for me. I became almost hysterical with the fear that he would be forgotten. It really was an irrational fear since our son David bears Bill's middle name and his son Owen has William as his middle name. I needed more than that. Bill was an architect. When he died, at his wake, instead of photographs of him, we placed drawings of buildings he designed. We also included a quote from early twentieth-century American architect Julia Morgan: "My buildings will be my legacy . . . they will speak for me long after I'm gone."[22] This was the sentiment that I wanted memorialized. One of Bill's proudest accomplishments was that he designed five buildings for the Roxbury Latin School in Boston. After discussing my wishes with the development office at the school, they suggested an etched bronze plaque with the words,

---

20. Pipher, *Women Rowing North*, 76.
21. Whipple, *Lesbian Widows: Invisible Grief*, 149.
22. BrainyQuote, "My buildings will be."

"In memory of William D. Buckingham, Architect of the School from 1986 to 2002." The plaque is in the Smith Arts Center. The school has also agreed to put Bill's original drawings of the school buildings in the on-campus archives. This school has existed since 1645, so I guess I can put to rest the fear that my husband will be forgotten and continue on my own upward spiral.

Chapter 5

Spiritual Development

THERE IS CONSENSUS AMONG contemporary writers that in a normal adult, spirituality changes in mid-life. There is no exact definition of when that occurs, but there is the shared observation that at some point the goals and meaning of life change. The first half of life is outward focused, while as we age we become more inward focused. Adulthood begins with the establishment of identity through career, relationships, and acquisitions. At some point, perhaps at retirement or when children leave home or after a significant loss, we begin to question that identity, our goals, and all that stuff we have accumulated.

Margaret Guenther (1929–2016), an Episcopal priest, spiritual director, and retreat leader who had been professor of ascetical theology at General Theological Seminary in New York, defines the second half of life as "when we are finally grown up (which is not the same as ceasing to grow)."[1] She states further, "In the second half of life our perspective changes, and we are amazed to realize that some things just don't matter any more."[2] She describes the second half of life as a time of fruition, a spiritual fecundity that has nothing to do with human biology. It is also a time to embrace ambiguity.

1. Guenther, *Holy Ground*, loc. 121.
2. Guenther, *Holy Ground*, loc. 132.

Guenther writes about needing a new saint to accompany her in the second half of life. "I was looking for strong women who somehow kept their feet on solid ground even as they trusted God's mysterious current to bear them up, strong women who managed to live to full maturity and die in their beds."[3] Her solution is Saint Anne, affectionately known as Jesus's grandmother. Although Anne was greatly venerated in the Middle Ages, especially in Germany, she is not mentioned in canonical scripture. Guenther tells us that St. Anne was a patron of artisans and crafters. As Guenther discusses this, she says the following, which has timeless application:

> The second half of life is a time of craft and skill, a time when we may reorder and even recreate our lives. It is a crisis, a turning-point, neither good nor bad in itself, a time of cleared vision when we move purposefully off-centre and say "yes" to new ways of being alive.[4]

Helen Luke (1904–1995), an English Jungian analyst who founded Apple Farm Community in Michigan, bases her book *Old Age* on the stories of three characters of great literature: Odysseus, Lear, and Prospero. In the foreword, Thomas Moore notes that "the beauty of this book is that it isn't so much about aging as about the soul's process, its ongoing alchemy, responding to changes in the body, in life, and in one's sense of self."[5] In the introduction, Barbara A. Mowat sees us faced with a choice between two directions:

> One path is tempting us toward repetition of our life's triumphs, tempting us toward wreckage and the inferno, the other coaxing us toward the true journey of the soul that has lived long and well, and that must turn away from mere continuation of accustomed efforts to new, significant, perhaps painful, soul journeys to plant oars in desert lands and to offer in sacrifice our past strengths and triumphs.[6]

3. Guenther, *Holy Ground*, loc.199.
4. Guenther, *Holy Ground*, loc. 48.
5. Luke, *Old Age*, loc. 41.
6. Luke, *Old Age*, loc. 93.

Spiritual Development

Luke herself speaks of the two paths when telling the story of King Lear: "We use the term *growing old* indiscriminately about those who are in truth growing into old age, into the final flowering and meaning of their lives, and about those who are being dragged into it, protesting, resisting, crying out against their inevitable imprisonment."[7]

For those who embrace the challenge it can be said that while the physical sphere of our life diminishes, our understanding of the meaning of life expands. We are able to embrace ambiguity and put things in perspective. In what may seem scary to younger people, we are able to face the inevitability of death with equanimity and sometimes even anticipation.

Like Helen Luke, the Franciscan author Richard Rohr talks about integrating what we learn in the first half of life into the wisdom of the second half of life.

> The language of the first half of life and the language of the second half of life are almost two different vocabularies, known only to those who have been in both of them. ... If you cannot include and integrate the wisdom of the first half of life, I doubt if you have moved to the second. ... People who know how to creatively break the rules also know why the rules were there in the first place. They are not mere iconoclasts or rebels.[8]

Bill's terminal diagnosis was more shocking to me than his actual death. I always expected to be a widow, but not before I turned seventy. In May of 2013 he visited the doctor because he was often finding himself short of breath. Pulmonary fibrosis is easily detected by a stethoscope during a routine physical exam. It produces a crackling sound in the lungs. When his primary care practitioner detected this, we were immediately sent to see a pulmonologist. That doctor prescribed further testing and eventually a lung biopsy that resulted in a week in the hospital. The prognosis was three to five years. Bill died eighteen months after his diagnosis.

7. Luke, *Old Age*, loc. 400.
8. Rohr, *Falling Upward*, loc. 449.

Mary Pipher, the author of *Women Rowing North*, speaks about wisdom being one of the spiritual gifts of the second half of life:

> My premise is that there is an amazing calculus at play in this developmental stage. The more that is taken from us, the more capacity we have for compassion and appreciation. Growth requires healing from tragedies and integrating them into our own wholeness. Though we have lost a great deal, we can strive to become women who experience a great appreciation for life. One of the great paradoxes of this life stage is that we experience not only the largest number of catastrophes but also the highest well-being. Our contentment comes from acceptance of life as it is. Wisdom compensates for our travails. We can navigate the river's snags, logjams, and downpours with competence and confidence. We can explore the mysteries along the river of time that we help each other travel down.[9]

James Hollis, writing in *Finding Meaning in the Second Half of Life*, states,

> A mature spirituality requires a mature individual. A mature spirituality already lies within each of us in our potential to take on the Mystery as it comes to us, to query it, to risk change and growth, and to continue the revisioning of our journey for so long as we live. It remains to be seen how ready we are to take the step toward this responsibility for personal authority.[10]

Subtitled *Opening the Eight Gates of Wisdom*, Angeles Arrien's book *The Second Half of Life* reinforces and extends the ideas of the writers quoted above:

> The second half of life is the ultimate initiation. In it, we encounter new, unexpected, unfamiliar, and unknowable moments that remind us that we are a sacred mystery made manifest. If we truly understand what is required

---

9. Pipher, *Women Rowing North*, loc. 467.
10. Hollis, *Finding Meaning*, 206.

Spiritual Development

of us at this stage, we are blessed with an enormous opportunity to develop and embody wisdom and character. We enjoyed limitless possibilities to restore, renew and heal ourselves, and because of our increased longevity for the first time in history, we also have the opportunity to create a map of spiritual maturity for future generations to use as they enter their own later years.[11]

Another truth that has been voiced by so many is also stressed by Rohr: "Only through great love or great suffering do we access the greatest spiritual teachings."[12] It is easy to see that many widows are likely to have experienced both.

---

11. Arrien, *Second Half of Life*, 4.
12. Rohr, *Falling Upward*, loc. 443.

Chapter 6

The Widows Speak

ONE OF THE REQUIREMENTS for my master of applied spirituality degree was to interview between four and six people. My five interviews were conducted individually in April and May of 2022 over Zoom. All of the women I interviewed are American, living in the United States. At the time of the interviews they were between sixty and eighty years of age. Their spouses had died at least two years before the interviews took place. None of the women had remarried.

 The interviews were recorded as they occurred and subsequently transcribed. The transcripts were returned to those interviewed for confirmation, corrections, comments, and omissions. The interviews were semi-structured. The following questions served as a guide. The women were so eager to share their stories that often the topics were covered before the questions were needed.

SAMPLE QUESTIONNAIRE FOR INDIVIDUAL INTERVIEWS

History: How Did You Become a Widow?

When did your partner die?
How long were you married?
Was it a sudden death?
If after an illness, how long?
Were you prepared for your partner's death?
If yes, in what way were you prepared?

Spiritual Life Before Widowhood

For purposes of this study spirituality is NOT the same as religion. Spirituality is everything related to the ultimate dimensions of beauty, truth, goodness, meaning, and love.

Did you belong to a formal religious tradition?
If yes, what was your involvement?
Would you describe yourself as spiritual, but not religious?
Were you involved in any creative activities?
If yes, what were those activities?
Were you a member of a group that met regularly?

Spiritual Life After Widowhood

What kind of ceremony, if any, marked your spouse's passing?
Did you participate in a bereavement group?

Did spirituality play a part in your grief resolution?

How has your spirituality changed since the death of your partner?

How have your activities changed since the death of your partner?

What activities helped you through your grief?

Are there any other factors that you think may have influenced the resolution of your grief?

ANNE'S STORY

When I first met Dr. Anne Silver she was affiliated professor of spiritual direction at General Theological Seminary in New York and the director of the Center for Christian Spirituality at that same location. She had come to General in 2007 to develop and teach courses in spiritual direction and lay ministry.

Anne's husband, David, died on April 24, 2003, after a long battle with cancer. They had been married for almost twenty-four years. David had children and grandchildren from previous marriages; Anne and David had no children together. She lives alone in one of the five boroughs of New York in the same house where she and her husband lived.

Dr. Silver said that all her energy had gone into her marriage and she didn't regret it by any means. But once David died, that energy was freed up to go to other things. Anne declined to be identified by a pseudonym. She said that her life is an open book. That is literally true. Her contribution to the book *Where You Go, I Shall* is about her life before and after her husband died.

Both the literature and the personal interviews stress the importance of social support for widows. That support could be in the form of an intentional bereavement group, caring family and friends, or a close-knit faith community. Mary Ellen Doherty writes, "The findings suggest that social support from family, friends, and colleagues aids widows by facilitating their embeddedness in a social network."[1]

None of the women I interviewed had joined bereavement groups, yet all of them spoke eloquently about the support they received from close friends and family.

Anne didn't attend a bereavement group per se, but her work on the book *Where You Go, I Shall* required regular intense meetings with her two coauthors. She found that very helpful and supportive. This is how she explained it during our interview:

> It turned into this wonderful healing experience because I was writing with two other people, one of whom also was a widow, and another person was a clergy person writing about the biblical pieces. And I would say that was the first really amazing spiritual experience after my husband died. That experience of intense community working on something like this. And it was within the first year after he died.
>
> So the experience of writing a book about this was probably the most healing experience I could possibly have, because not only was I dealing with this, but writing is my thing. Writing is my voice. Writing is my preferred art modality. This was so perfect. And then to have this whole community experience where we're writing together, we'd all three of us sit down at somebody's dining room table and just go over the drafts of things. So it was a very communal writing experience and so it was prayerful. We prayed at the beginning, we prayed at the end. It was just so intense and then sharing it with others once the book got published was interesting, too.[2]

Since her retirement from teaching at General Seminary, Anne has continued to offer individual spiritual direction. She also conducts retreats and quiet days on topics such as "Finding God in All Things," "Finding Sabbath in Ministry," "Grieving: From Isolation to Community," and "Biblical and Modern Images of Widowhood." To her delight, this allows Anne the best parts of teaching,

1. Doherty and Scannell-Desch, "Post-Traumatic Growth," 85.
2. Anne Silver, interview with the author, Apr. 25, 2022.

which she loved, without the administrative responsibilities and the drudgery, intensity, and stress of grading.

CREATIVITY AS SALVATION

Abigail is a retired Episcopal priest who was married to another priest who was twenty-two years older than she. They were married for thirty years before he died from complications of prostate cancer. Each of them had children and grandchildren from previous marriages. She continues to live in the last home that they shared: a two-family house that they co-owned with Abigail's daughter, her husband, and their two young children, all of whom live upstairs.

During the interviews, the first question I asked was "How did your husband die?"

> When I married my husband, I knew that I would most likely be burying him because he was so much older. My husband was twenty-two years older than me. But Ron brought into my life experiences that I never would have had with anyone else. By that I mean my trips to Italy, learning to speak Italian, but not as well as he did. Our life was, at least in my memory, fairy-tale like. His death, although I knew it was going to be coming—I didn't know what the experience would be like. So when he was diagnosed with cancer of the prostate and that had metastasized, I started feeling panic, really panic. Like, what am I going to do, and what am I going to do after he's gone? So Ron not only was part of my spiritual energy and intellectual life, but he cooked. He was my house husband because he was so much older, and he was a very fine cook. When we first got married, we were trading off three days. What we discovered is that I would be cooking, heating up his meals on my days. Finally I said, you know, I'll clean, you cook. And that's where it went for thirty years.

For Abigail *making* provided a means of channeling the energy from her marriage into productive activity that helped her resolve her grief. She designs and makes many of her own clothes. At one point she began making soft dolls that represent characters. Often she is commissioned to make specific ones for people. More recently, Abigail is designing and making custom jackets out of used Indian saris. She has had great success selling these items at craft fairs and art festivals. Her interview continued,

> I just spoke to my brother, whom I haven't talked to in a year. He and I are very similar. I said I feel like I'm dead unless I'm making something or planning to make something. For me that's sewing or painting.
>
> My brother is into mechanics and he's building a car and building this and that and the other thing. So that's the reason I am hellbent on converting my garage into an artist studio because my faith is sitting right there. It's on the canvas. It's in my sewing machine. And ideas flow in and out of my head. Ron never understood my need to create artistically so it was a part of me that I didn't develop much when we were together. Now I feel like I'm trying to make up for lost time. I'm not quite sure how those two things are threaded together, but they are. They definitely are. And I feel trapped in my little room with my little canvases, and I just want to go big. I feel like God has put something in me, and I have not yet played with that talent.

KAREN'S HAPPY ENDING

Karen met her husband Dave when she was seventeen and they were both in college. They married and moved to New England when he was offered a position in the physics department at a local college. He stayed in that job until he died in January 2019. They had been married over fifty years but never had children. Karen worked as the manager of an independent book store in a neighboring town. One night when they were out to dinner, Dave slipped and fell while crossing the street. He was rushed to the hospital where it was determined that he had broken his hip. Complications ensued, and Dave died two weeks after his fall.

Karen pointed out one positive result of Dave's quick death. Her memories of her husband are not of months of intense caregiving like many others who nursed their husbands through long terminal illnesses. Her memories are of Dave as vital and strong rather than of him being an invalid. This is what she said:

> You have to deal with that shock, which is a whole different thing than something that you know is coming. I've been with people who have been sick for a long time and died, and I've been with them when they died. It's just a very different experience. And yet when I think about him, it's not about the last year of his life being a long, drawn out, painful, whatever thing, like so many people that I know have gone through. I've talked to a couple of friends who had a partner who died from cancer and said they so often think of the last year and they wish they didn't have to think of that.

Vicky Whipple echoes these differences:

> Both sudden and prolonged deaths are tragic and hurt deeply. The difference between a sudden death and one that has been anticipated is not in the amount of pain that we feel but in the ability to prepare for the death. I know that I began grieving from the moment I heard about Em's fatal diagnosis. Those who lost their partner unexpectedly experienced the same kind of pain at the moment they were told that their partner had died, but they were deprived of the opportunity I had to prepare for Emily's death and say good-bye. On the other hand, they did not have to watch their partner waste away and suffer over an extended period.[3]

For me the shock of my husband's terminal diagnosis was more painful than his actual death, which was very peaceful. He was not seventy years old and was still working full-time in the profession that he loved when he was told he had pulmonary fibrosis. It was the end of our dreams of extensive travel and of watching

---

3. Whipple, *Lesbian Widows: Invisible Grief*, 16.

grandchildren grow. I always expected to be a widow some day, but not before I turned seventy!

During the early stages of the COVID lockdowns, Karen found much help, especially from friends and neighbors. One neighbor did her grocery shopping every week for a full year. She was surprised and delighted by the actions of previously casual acquaintances who came forward with concrete measures of support. Conversely she was disappointed when some of the people she would have expected to be supportive weren't.

I mentioned to Karen that the literature explained how some people avoided widows because the widows reminded them how fragile life is and they preferred to avoid that realization. Also, some women saw the widow, now a single woman, as temptation to their husbands. Karen then recounted an incident where the wife of a couple that she and her husband had known since college days told the woman's children that Karen had been "really hot" in college, that lots of men pursued her, even their father. Karen saw this as fear on the part of her friend that the husband might renew his interest in her.

Five years after her husband's death, Karen is now in a new relationship with a man who was a colleague of her husband. About two years ago, Jack called to speak with Dave, not knowing that Dave had died. Jack lived in another part of the country. Karen explained the situation and Jack shared that his wife had also died. They had a long conversation about their experiences of bereavement and their current lives. Unlike Karen, Jack has children and grandchildren. Since that first conversation Karen and Jack have continued to talk and now share a video conference call every evening when they are not together. Karen has met Jack's family and Jack has met Karen's friends. During the first year of their relationship they spent about one week out of every month in either of their homes or in a third location.

When I recently spoke with Karen, she said that they are trying to cut down on their travel time—they are both in their eighties—by seeing each other less frequently but for longer visits. Neither of them has any desire to sell their current house and actually live together. Karen understands that Jack wants to be near his children and grandchildren. If she sold her house and moved in with him and then he died, she would be in an unfamiliar location with only Jack's relatives as support. For now they see each other for three weeks out of each month and spend one week alone in their own house. They both consider themselves very lucky to have formed this relationship.

STAYING STRONG FOR HER SON

Nonnie is the youngest of the women interviewed. She married late in life and has a son, Ian, who was twelve years old at the time of our initial interview. She just turned sixty. Her husband, John, was fourteen years older than she was. They had been married for twelve years when he died in 2016 of pulmonary fibrosis. She continues to live in the house that she bought before she met her husband, where she has a home office from which she conducts a business. When I asked Nonnie if she had joined a bereavement group, this was her answer:

> I did not, because I didn't think I'd be able to get through it. No, I didn't. I thought about it, but for a good year or two, Margery, I cried a lot. I couldn't help it. It was like somebody turned the switch and the tears came even unknowing to me. It just started and I couldn't help it. Ian would come into the kitchen or wherever I was, and he'd see me crying, and he'd walk out of the room and I'd say, "Honey, I'm sorry. I can't help it." And he saw me so many times, and I thought a bereavement group . . . If I couldn't talk about it with my friends and family, how am I going to talk about it with strangers?

I then asked, "So where did you find support in those first couple of years?"

> I found support mostly in my friends. Okay. Yeah, mostly in my friends. Plus I stayed home. I didn't want to see anybody. I didn't get together with people. Lots of support over the phone. I had a certain couple of friends that

I go out with. If I cried in front of them, it was okay. I wasn't comfortable doing that with everybody, so I just didn't see people. Ian and I just formed our little cocoon and it was okay, just us. It's how I had to deal with it.

When I asked Nonnie, "Do you think you would marry again?" She gave a very detailed answer:

You know, I don't know the answer to that. Yeah. I mean, I just turned sixty on New Year's Eve. And when I think about it, if I ever found someone, they're going to be in their sixties and I don't want to go through that again. I don't want to get so close to somebody that I'm going to have to take care of them and they're going to die on me again. So right now I say, "No." I'm comfortable with Ian and me. I'm very sad to think he's going to go to college and I'm going to be here all alone. A part of me thinks, well, maybe you should have somebody here. But then I think of the sickness part, and I don't want to do it again.

The last time I spoke to Nonnie, her son was heading into his junior year in high school. He is doing very well with a 4.15 GPA because he is taking advanced classes. As proud as she is of him, she dreads when he will leave home for college. She has already told him that in order for her to pay his tuition and expenses he must choose one of the 262 schools in New England, ideally one that is no more than a two-hour drive from where they currently live outside of Boston.

DÉJÀ VU (PATRICIA'S STORY)

Patricia is a seventy-one-year-old member of a large extended family that gets together often. She has four sisters, three brothers, and numerous nieces and nephews. She is especially close to her next older sister, Marie, who is a medical professional. Patricia's husband, Edward, to whom she was married for forty-one years, died in 2018 from complications due to diabetes and heart problems. Over the years he had two heart attacks and quadruple bypass surgery. They have two adult children.

> I got the sickness part along with the health part. I'm sure if you printed out his file, it would fill a bookshelf. There was always a health episode going on with him. That continued to escalate in seriousness. I had retired the year before he died in order to spend more time with him. I can't say that I had a resurgence of energy after he died. The grief I experienced was very different from what I expected to feel. I thought I would be stronger knowing his death was imminent, but that wasn't the reality. I thought, "How would I move on from this devastating loss?" What did I do with my time? I don't know. I think I just got deeper into the things that I had always enjoyed doing, like my crafting. I always call it my art therapy. I think being able to make things, to escape into art, I was able to devote more of my time and energy in a positive direction. Creating beautiful things brought me peace.

Patricia referred to a quote attributed to Pablo Picasso that she has framed in her home. "Art washes away from the soul the dust of everyday life."[4] She hasn't sold her work commercially, but justifies it as "art therapy." She does give her creations to friends and family who treasure these gifts and encourage her to go public.

> When someone you love dies, you revisit every other death that you lived through. Much of what I experienced with Edward was emotionally like reliving my time with my daughter, Erin. I knew from the day she was born that she was dying. Every day I would say, "Is today the day?" Ultimately it was that day. As horrible as I felt both times, I think I also felt relief in knowing that when I wake up from now on, I won't have to say, "Is today the day?"
>
> I don't like the expression "to bring closure." I understand the importance of rituals in the grief process, but I don't like the expression "well, now they are in a better place." They've had a funeral. To me, there is no closure. You cannot consider these events in your life ever closed. You can't move on without feeling the impact on your

---

4. Like many others, Patricia mistakenly attributed this quote to Pablo Picasso. The correct reference should be to Berthold Auerbach (Auerbach, *On the Heights*, 64).

life. And so to me, closure means, I'm done with that and move on. I think that's a cold statement. I mean, I get the process. I think it's the terminology that throws me. I don't have closure to the major traumatic events in my life, I adapt them into my life.

Patricia is currently working fifteen hours a week as visitor services coordinator at an historic house museum in her home town. Her major was museum studies in the bachelor's degree that she earned by attending night school for many years while working full-time as a medical technician. She loves giving tours to the visitors and working with the seventeenth-century artifacts on display in the house. Currently she is planning a cooking demonstration using recipes from the house's archives.

> Many studies suggest that engaging in art and creative activities can have physiological effects that reduce stress and promote well-being. Whether through formal art therapy programs or informal creative hobbies, incorporating creativity into a stress management routine can be a beneficial way to reduce stress levels. . . . The power of creativity to reduce stress is multifaceted. From providing outlets for self-expression to inducing meditative flow states, creative pursuits offer a diverse number of stress-reduction benefits. They enable us to reframe perspectives, regulate emotions, and engage in calming practices that ground us in the present moment.[5]

---

5. MQ Mental Health, "Art of Destressing."

Chapter 7

After-Death Communication

ONGOING COMMUNICATION WITH DECEASED loved ones is a common, but rarely discussed, practice among bereaved people. My current work aims to bring this phenomenon from the obscurity of academic journals into public conversation.

Interest in this topic began for me during research for my master's dissertation, "Growing through Grief: Widowhood as a Catalyst for Spiritual Development," at SETU in Waterford, Ireland. Each of the women I interviewed described experiences of communication with their deceased husbands. These encounters took various forms—dreams, sensory experiences, unexplained coincidences, messages from mutual friends, and animal embodiment of the spirit of the dead person.

This chapter gives an overview of how ongoing relationships with the deceased have been viewed in twentieth-century bereavement studies and how these views have changed with the emergence of continuing-bonds perspective. The work and ideas of Edith Maria Steffen, Lytta Basset, Dennis Klass, and Cynthia Bourgeault, among others, are discussed.

The dominant view that ongoing connections with deceased loved ones are a sign of pathology can be traced to Freud's famous paper "Mourning and Melancholia" (1917). Here, Freud proposed that the goal of grief was the relinquishing of the bond with the deceased in order to become free to engage in new relationships.[1]

More recently, attitudes toward grief resolution have been influenced by study of continuing bonds. No longer are people encouraged to sever ties to the deceased. Instead, they are encouraged to incorporate past relationships into revised identities that acknowledge trauma and grief and seek to grow from these experiences.

This revised view emerged toward the end of the twentieth century. Rooted in insights from non-Western cultures, the seminal publication of *Continuing Bonds: New Understandings of Grief* by Klass, Silverman, and Nickman in 1996 signaled a paradigm shift in bereavement research and practice, as it revolutionized the landscape with its key message that continuing our relationships with the deceased is normal and can be positive even for the deceased.[2]

Edith Maria Steffen, a major voice on this topic, explains that these connections were once viewed negatively, but now more positively. She summarizes her findings in the following abstract:

> This chapter looks at different ways of making sense of continuing bonds and seeks to address what role religious beliefs and particularly afterlife beliefs may play in ongoing relationships with deceased loved ones and specifically in how anomalous or extraordinary experiences of the deceased are perceived and made sense of. Here a perspective on grief was taken that marked a shift from viewing relating to the dead as prohibited or evil to a view that relating to the dead is pathological. E. R. Benore and C. L. Park have suggested that experiences such as sensory and quasi-sensory experiences of the deceased may have a facilitative function in post-loss meaning-making. Sense of presence experiences seem to involve an awareness of or a relationship with a transcendent reality, i.e. a reality beyond ordinary experience.[3]

1. Freud, *On Murder*, 203–14.
2. Klass et al., *Continuing Bonds*.
3. Steffen, "Continuing Bonds," abstract.

Patricia has had visitation experiences with each of her lost loved ones. Months after the baby died she dreamed that she was standing in the kitchen. Since Erin had only lived for four months, she would never have been standing at that age. Patricia interpreted this to mean that her daughter was now happy. This is exactly what Black, Murkar, and Black are explaining:

> Frequently reported dream images during the grief process include having the dreamer awaken with a feeling that they have had actual contact with the spirit of the deceased. The sensation of having contact with the deceased can lead the bereaved to awaken with a deep sense of awe, self-renewal, and a feeling of peace. These "visitation" type dreams can be beneficial in one's adjustment after the loss, as the dreams can both promote a deeper conviction of life after death and assist in finding personal meaning.[4]

With her husband, the visitation was not a dream, but a feeling of his presence about a year and a half after he died. They had loved to dance at weddings. One day Patricia heard a song on the radio and thought, "That would be a good song to dance to." She immediately had the sensation that Edward was with her and they were dancing. Both of these visitation experiences have given her comfort and reassurance about her lost loved ones.

> It's corny. But I heard a piece of music that I said, oh, that sounds like a nice piece of music that you would dance to, like at a wedding or something. We used to dance whenever we went to a wedding. So I was thinking about him, and then all of a sudden, I felt that he was with me and dancing, that I could fantasize that we were dancing. We didn't do it often, but whenever we could, we danced, and I always enjoyed that dancing with him, slow dancing. That's the only time. It wasn't a piece of music that we had ever heard together. It was new music. And I just thought, oh, that's a nice song. You know, that would be nice to dance with him to that song. And then all of a

---

4. Black et al., "Examining the Healing Process," 11.

sudden, I felt weird in a good way. But that's the only contact experience that I've had.

Karen also recounted both dreams and physical experiences.

> Well, I do have dreams about him. I didn't for a long time. I would say for the first six months, maybe I never had a dream about him. And I kept wishing I would. But after that, I started having dreams, and I still do. It's not often. Occasionally. Sometimes I have dreams where both of my parents are in the dreams and they've both been dead now, my dad for almost twelve years and my mom for three. For the first—God, how long did it last? Six months, maybe—I would sit on the couch in the room where the television is, and the chair that Dave sat in was right next to the couch. I would have this sense of somebody sitting in that chair, and then I would look and of course, nobody would be in the chair. When I wake up in the morning, like, for the first fifteen seconds I was awake, I would reach over and think, and then I would think like, oh, yeah, right.

Anne recounted a dream that a close friend had related to Anne's late sister:

> A couple of weeks after my sister died, one of our best friends emailed me and said, "I've got to tell you about this dream that I had." And she described this dream where my sister was young and well and whole and happy, and she'd never seen her like that. She'd only seen her in a wheelchair in a nursing home. She'd never seen this version of my sister. And she said she sometimes has experiences like that with people who have died. She probably has a thinner veil between the two worlds than most of us since it wasn't an unusual experience for her. And I thought, okay, thank you. Since I had asked my sister to do that, too.

In her contribution to *Where You Go, I Shall*, Anne describes a joyful encounter with her deceased husband:

> For the first year after he died, David almost never appeared in my dreams. But the night after the conversation with my friends, I dreamed I was attending a relative's wedding in a synagogue that had many beautiful, ornate rooms. The ceremony was to be performed by the rabbi who had conducted David's funeral. All of a sudden, David showed up to join me! He was well and whole, and everyone seemed quite matter-of-fact about his being there, even though it was known that he had died. Eventually, because the rabbi was so late in arriving, David started leading us toward the door. I told him I wasn't ready to leave yet, so we stayed and talked about photography for the rest of the dream. It was delightful to have him with me again![5]

All of the interviewed widows and the literature speak of forgetting for a moment that the spouse has died and wanting to share something with them before remembering that they are gone. Some of us still talk to our husbands and expect that they are listening and can intervene and advocate on our behalf.

Nonnie derives great comfort from mourning doves.

> I was trying to design his headstone, I wanted it to be really nice. It's a very hard thing to design. So I had finally found this one design after searching many on the Internet. My tombstone guy sent it out to a person to draw it because it was a very kind of delicate scene. So the day that he sent it to me by email so I could approve it, a couple of weeks prior to that, maybe a month prior, these two birds came to live in our house, and we didn't know what they were. And the day that the person sent it to me for approval, I was having coffee in the kitchen with my sister here, and something banged off the window on the side deck. We went out to look, and it was one of those birds laying on the deck. The other bird, the mate, was in the tree watching. So we started to call up places because we didn't want them to die because we love the animals. Come to find out, they're mourning doves.

---

5. Parkerton, *Where You Go*, 99.

Ian had a play date that day, and that boy's father was a cardiologist. He came to get him, and I said, Paul, this is what happened. There's a bird. What can we do? We went on the deck to find him. The bird was gone. So I opened the email from the person doing the tombstone design and what I had chosen, which I didn't know at the time, were mourning doves!

During Christmas time I went outside with the dog, and there's a tree right here next to the deck. And there were about twenty-five mourning doves sleeping in the tree that morning. I took pictures. I have them on my phone. I had Ian come out and look, and it was amazing. And to me, that's a sign. And it's pretty cool when we see them on the sidewalk when we walk around the block. We say, "John, go home now." We don't want anything to happen to them. We want them to come back.

Some believe that the meaning of a mourning dove is a visit or sign of encouragement from a friend or family member. Doves provide comfort because they help people remember their loved ones are watching over them. The birds' soft cooing song and romantic behavior toward their mates send a powerful energy of love.[6] This is especially true in Celtic, Native American, Chinese, and African cultures. The doves represent love, hope, peace, and good fortune.[7]

Lytta Basset is a Swiss theologian. Since her academic retirement in 2017 she has been the editor of the University of Neuchâtel's international theology journal, *La chair et le soufflé (The Flesh and the Breath)*.

In 2001, Basset's son, a Protestant pastor and theologian whose entire work was centered on the notion of misfortune, committed suicide at the age of twenty-four. For several months, she took daily note of the events and feelings that inhabited her. With hindsight, she comments on her notes and tries to interpret them in the light of psychology and the Gospels.

---

6. Matthias, "Dove Meaning," item 3.
7. David, "Spiritual Meaning of Doves," paras. 6–15.

In 2007, she wrote in *Ce lien qui ne meurt jamais* (*The Bond That Never Dies*) how her son came into communication with her, according to a phenomenon identified as subjective contact with the deceased (vécus subjectifs de contact avec un défunt—VSCD). In a later book, *This Beyond That Makes Us a Sign*, released at the end of 2022, she reveals the unlikely event at the origin of her contacts with Samuel: powerful messages from her son received by one of his students, named Myriam, during a university course abroad.

> No book has cost me so much. His matrix is a diary that I undertook to keep from the first weeks of mourning, after the suicide of our 24-year-old son Samuel.... Five years later, I took up elements of this autobiographical document by writing them in the third person, and accompanying them with Meditations or reflections formulated in "I". Already, I had begun to publicly address these subjects that remained largely taboo in our Western societies: death, suicide, the afterlife, our relationship to invisible realities.... The path of truth that leads to a Life stronger than the irreparable is not to the prerogative of believers. The cleavage is elsewhere. It depends on the orientation chosen: despite or through the death of a loved one, do we ardently desire to go towards what lives or do we decide to stifle this Desire?[8]

While weaving the links between the Bible, the VSCD phenomenon, science, and her personal experiences, Lytta Basset describes a journey that made her "love life even more."[9]

Cynthia Bourgeault is an Episcopal priest who worked closely with Fr. Thomas Keating, founder of the Centering Prayer movement, and Fr. Richard Rohr, prolific author and director of the Center for Action and Contemplation in Albuquerque, New Mexico. In 2021 she was named to the Watkins List of the hundred most spiritually influential people in the world.

---

8. Basset, *Cet au-delà*, 9.
9. Basset, "Interview."

After-Death Communication

In her book *Love Is Stronger Than Death: The Mystical Union of Two Souls* (2014), she tells the story of her relationship with Brother Raphael Robin, "Rafe," a seventy-year-old Trappist monk and hermit. Both believed that a relationship can continue beyond this life. She describes her search for that connection before and after Rafe's death.

> Once early on, as I was struggling to sort out in my mind the confusing and sketchy details of his life, I suddenly heard him say, "Quit it! It's useless to rummage about in my life. Who I was in life was incomplete. Instead, accept who I am now—what I am growing into."[10]

Bourgeault says that she never had visual experiences of Rafe, but in addition to hearing him often, she also describes an experience where he writes to her: "To my astonishment, at the end of an intense morning of prayer, I found myself writing in my journal, the pen literally streaming out in front of me." The essence of what he wrote was, "Let yourself be loved."[11]

In a subsequent book Cynthia Bourgeault talks about another man whose name was Johnny the Greek, a fisherman in Maine with whom she had a relationship.[12] He had a catamaran, and they went to the Caribbean sailing. What follows is a concrete illustration of consolation and desolation as defined in Ignatian spirituality. If you're trying to make a decision and things are going smoothly, that's usually a confirmation that you're on the right path. If things keep going wrong, that shows you're not on the right path. The ocean journey was one disaster after another. The final straw was when the mast broke, the boat sank, and they escaped with just their lives. They both knew it was time to heed the signs and end the relationship. With a broken heart Cynthia went back to teaching and writing and Johnny continued to sail alone.[13] The book is dedicated to Johnny.

---

10. Bourgeault, *Love Is Stronger*, 99.
11. Bourgeault, *Love Is Stronger*, 100.
12. Bourgeault, *Eye of the Heart*, 8.
13. Bourgeault, *Eye of the Heart*, 6–10.

In her book about lesbian widows, Dr. Victoria Whipple, a clinical member and approved supervisor for the American Association for Marriage and Family Therapy, writes, "Another typical experience, especially in the first few months after the death of a loved one, is to have a sense of our deceased partner's presence and to talk to her as if she were still alive."[14] Whipple also states that dreams of the deceased help us to do grief work at an unconscious level.

The current state of continuing conversations has been compared to that of near-death experiences (NDEs) fifty years ago. At that time NDEs were suspect. American psychiatrist Raymond Moody coined the term *near-death experience* in 1975 in his bestselling book *Life After Life*.[15] Since then, this phenomenon has been the subject of much research and is no longer considered fringe investigation. Numerous first-person accounts have been published. One can predict a similar trajectory for continuing bonds and direct after-death communication. This can happen if we change the conversation around grief and bereavement from one with a goal of closure to one of a revised, ongoing relationship with our deceased loved ones.

---

14. Whipple, *Lesbian Widows: Invisible Grief*, 100.
15. Moody, *Life After Life*, 175.

Appendix

How Friends and Family Can Help

THE MOST HELPFUL THING you can do to help someone who is in mourning is to listen without judgment. Bereaved people need to talk. If you knew the person they are grieving, you can share your memories of that person. Avoid cliches like "They're in a better place," or "We all die eventually." While that is true, it doesn't help when a person is experiencing a recent loss.

Refrain from making broad or undefined general statements like "Please let me know if there's anything I can do for you." Instead, offer something specific such as doing a load of laundry, bringing dinner, walking the dog, or accompanying the bereaved to the place of worship to plan the funeral or celebration of life. Writing thank-you notes for flowers or donations can be a lonely and stressful task. Helping or just being present to talk during this process would be greatly appreciated.

When my husband died our adult daughter made the arrangements to have his oxygen concentrator returned to the rental company. I didn't have to ask her, she just did it. One less thing for me to deal with. Our son packed up his father's clothes after selecting a few favorite ties to keep. He then took the rest to a donation center where they were happy to distribute them to people in need.

Appendix

I personally appreciated and agreed with one of the pieces of advice Bill Dodds lists in his book *On Your Pilgrimage Called Grief: A Guide for Widows and Widowers*.[1] He talks about how even the happiest moments can be tinged with sadness. Our son's wedding took place nine months after my husband died. Of course I was very happy for David and his bride, but I felt very alone and wished so much that Bill was there physically, even though I was assured by others that he was there in spirit.

When Patricia's husband died, she didn't want a traditional funeral but still wanted to honor his passing somehow with friends and family. She was very grateful when her two older sisters arranged their own version of the Jewish custom of sitting shiva. Patricia was deeply touched by the number of friends and relatives who attended, and by the memories of Edward that they shared with her.

If there are children involved, you can arrange activities that may distract them from all the sadness that they are experiencing. After checking with their caregiver, you may want to take them away from their home for a short time. Getting them involved in a creative activity may even allow them to talk about what they are experiencing. As always, you want to listen without judgement.

If the person died after a long illness, acknowledge what good care his partner took of him, or how faithfully she visited him in the hospital.

Saying nothing to the bereaved is probably the worst thing you can do. Many people never reach out because they don't know what to say, or they are afraid of saying something inappropriate. This is a mistake. Grieving people will be left bewildered thinking that you have abandoned them to suffer alone. "Expressing feelings of emptiness, isolation, and loneliness is taboo for some and terrifying for many; however, the last thing one needs is less conversation on this topic, as loneliness is pervasive, damaging to the human spirit, and even deadly."[2]

---

1. Dodds, *Pilgrimage Called Grief*, 138.
2. Saracino, "Intimate Wilderness," 173.

How Friends and Family Can Help

In some ways grieving is like being in labor during the birthing process—the only way out is through! Suppressed or denied grief festers. It can manifest physically and mentally, causing sleeping problems, tension, headaches, nausea, fatigue, and general malaise.

If you notice these symptoms in a bereaved friend or family member you might help them by engaging in a creative activity such as singing, dancing, or making art. This can help them channel the stuck emotions into something physical, allowing grief to move through them rather than remain suppressed. Expressing what you're feeling gives the body an opportunity to release pent-up emotions in a healthy way.

Remember to keep in touch after the "thud period," as Louise Woodruff calls it.[3] This is the time after the wake and funeral or memorial service are over and the widow finds herself alone in an empty dwelling. Weeks, months, and even years later the widow will appreciate your concern and thoughtfulness.

---

3. In conversation with the author, September 26, 2025.

Bibliography

Arrien, Angeles. *The Second Half of Life: Opening the Eight Gates of Wisdom.* Boulder, CO: Sounds True, 2007.

Auerbach, Berthold. *On the Heights.* Vol. 2. Translated by F. E. Bunnett. Leipzig: Bernhard Tauchnitz, 1867.

Basset, Lytta. *Ce lien qui ne meurt jamais.* Paris: Albin Michel, 2007.

———. *Cet au-delà qui nous fait signe.* Paris: Albin Michel, 2022.

———. "Interview with Lytta Basset." By Raphaël Zbinder. Cath.ch, March 6, 2023. https://www.cath.ch/newsf/lytta-basset-oui-on-peut-se-remettre-de-la-mort-dun-enfant/.

Bennett, Kate Mary. "Trajectories of Resilience Among Widows: A Latent Transition Model." *Aging and Mental Health* 24.12 (2020) 2014–21.

Bourgeault, Cynthia. *Eye of the Heart: A Spiritual Journey into the Imaginal Realm.* Boulder: Shambhala, 2020.

———. *Love Is Stronger Than Death: The Mystical Union of Two Souls.* New York: Monkfish, 1997.

BrainyQuote. "Julia Morgan Quotes." https://www.brainyquote.com/quotes/julia_morgan_193132.

Brown, Brené. *The Gifts of Imperfection.* Center City, MN: Hazelden, 2010.

Black, Joshua, et al. "Examining the Healing Process Through Dreams in Bereavement." *Sleep and Hypnosis* 16 (2014) 10–17.

David, Lauren. "The Spiritual Meaning of Doves and What to Do If They Keep Appearing." Mindbodygreen, Dec. 16, 2022. https://www.mindbodygreen.com/articles/dove-symbolism.

Dodds, Bill. *On Your Pilgrimage Called Grief: A Guide for Widows and Widowers.* Self-published, 2022.

Doherty, Mary Ellen, and Elizabeth Scannell-Desch. "Post-Traumatic Growth in Women Who Have Experienced the Loss of Their Spouse or Partner." *Nursing Forum* 57 (2022) 78–86. https://doi.org/10.1111/nuf.12657.

Eliot, T. S. *The Four Quartets.* New York: Houghton Mifflin, 1943. Kindle.

Flanagan, Bernadette, and Michael O'Sullivan. "Spirituality in Contemporary Ireland: Manifesting Indigeneity." *Spiritus: A Journal of Christian Spirituality* 16 (2016) 55–73.

BIBLIOGRAPHY

Frantz, Thomas T., et al. "Positive Outcomes of Losing a Loved One." In *Meaning Reconstruction and the Experience of Loss*, edited by Robert A. Neimeyer, 191–209. Washington, DC: American Psychological Association, 2001.

Freud, Sigmund. *On Murder, Mourning and Melancholia*. Translated by Shaun Whiteside. Penguin Classics. New York: Penguin, 2005.

Guenther, Margaret. *Toward Holy Ground*. Cambridge, MA: Cowley, 1995. Kindle.

Guilbert, Charles. *Book of Common Prayer*. New York: Oxford University Press, 1990.

Hollis, James. *Finding Meaning in the Second Half of Life*. New York: Avery, 2005.

Jerrard, Ronda. "Traditionally Widowhood Has Been Portrayed as a Positive Experience for Women. Was This the Case? II." *Queen Mary University History Journal*, July 14, 2021. https://qmhistoryjournal.wixsite.com/qmhj/post/traditionally-widowhood-has-been-portrayed-as-a-positive-experience-for-women-was-this-the-case-ii.

Kaveny, M. Cathleen. "The Order of Widows: What the Early Church Can Teach Us About Older Women and Health Care." *Christian Bioethics* 11 (2005) 11–34. https://www.tandfonline.com/doi/full/10.1080/13803600590926369.

Kessler, David. *Finding Meaning: The Sixth Stage of Grief*. New York: Scribner, 2019.

Klass, Dennis K., et al., eds. *Continuing Bonds: New Understandings of Grief*. New York: Routledge, 1996.

Kubler-Ross, Elisabeth. *On Death and Dying*. New York: Macmillan, 1969.

Luke, Helen. *Old Age*. New York: Parabola Books, 1987. Kindle.

Lupcho, Theresa. "Grief Vs. Mourning: Is There a Difference?" Thriveworks, Apr. 3, 2023. https://thriveworks.com/help-with/grief-loss/grief-vs-mourning/.

Matthias, Alice Knisley. "Dove Meaning: What Does It Mean If You See a Mourning Dove?" *Birds and Blooms*, Sept. 27, 2024. https://www.birdsandblooms.com/birding/birding-basics/mourning-dove-meaning/.

Miller, Christopher J. *The Spiritual Artist: We Are Designed to Create*. Independently published, 2020. Kindle.

Monbourquette, John. *How to Love Again: Moving from Grief to Growth*. London: Darton Longman & Todd, 2002.

Moody, Raymond. *Life After Life: The Bestselling Original Investigation That Revealed "Near-Death Experiences."* New York: HarperCollins, 2015.

Morgan, Stefana Borovska, et al. Abstract for "Spiritual Care: Profiles of Three Core Spiritual Needs in Older Patients with Advanced Cancer." *The American Journal of Geriatric Psychiatry* 23.3 (2015) S86–S87. https://doi.org/10.1016/j.jagp.2014.12.087.

MQ Mental Health. "The Art of Destressing: How Creativity Creates Less Stress." MQ Mental Health Research. Apr. 15, 2024. https://www.mqmentalhealth.org/the-art-of-destressing-how-creativity-creates-less-stress/.

Bibliography

Neimeyer, Robert A. "The Language of Loss: Grief Therapy as a Process of Meaning Reconstruction." In *Meaning Reconstruction and the Experience of Loss*, edited by Robert A. Neimeyer, 263–92. Washington DC: American Psychological Association, 2001.

Oxford English Dictionary. "Spirituality." https://www.oed.com/oedv2/00233694.

Parkerton, Jane J., et al. *Where You Go, I Shall: Gleanings from the Stories of Biblical Widows*. Cambridge, MA: Cowley, 2005.

Pipher, Mary. *Women Rowing North: Navigating Life's Currents and Flourishing As We Age*. New York: Bloomsbury, 2019. Kindle.

Psychology Today. "Spirituality." https://www.psychologytoday.com/us/basics/spirituality.

"Quote Origin: Showing Up Is 80 Percent of Life." June 10, 2013. https://quoteinvestigator.com/2013/06/10/showing-up/.

Rohr, Richard. *Falling Upward: A Spirituality for the Two Halves of Life*. AARP Digital Edition. Hoboken, NJ: Wiley & Sons, 2011.

Sanders, Catherine M. *Surviving Grief . . . and Learning to Live Again*. New York: Wiley & Sons, 1992.

Saracino, Michele. "Intimate Wilderness: A Spirituality of Empathy." *Spiritus* 21.2 (2021) 173–92.

Sheldrake, Philip. *A Brief History of Spirituality*, Hoboken, NJ: Wiley-Blackwell, 2007.

Smith, Scott L., Jr., ed. *The Interior Castle or the Mansions by St. Teresa of Avila*. Study Guide Edition. Translated by Benedict Zimmerman. New Roads, LA: Holy Water, 2024.

Steffen, Edith Maria. "Interacting with the Afterlife: Continuing Bonds with Deceased Loved Ones." In *Death, Immortality, and Eternal Life*, edited by T. Ryan Byerly, 11–27. London: Routledge, 2021. https://doi.org/10.4324/9781003058380.

Teilhard de Chardin, Pierre. *The Human Phenomenon*. Translated by Sarah Appleton-Weber. Brighton: Sussex Academic, 2021.

Tillich, Paul. *Systematic Theology*. Vol. 1. Chicago: University of Chicago Press, 1956.

Twain, Mark. *The Innocents Abroad or The New Pilgrims' Progress*. Hartford, CT: New York: Hippocrene, 1869. Google Books. https://www.google.com/books/edition/The_Innocents_Abroad/XX-wAAAAIAAJ.

Whipple, Vicky. *Lesbian Widows: Invisible Grief*. New York: Harrington Park, 2006. Kindle.

www.ingramcontent.com/pod-product-compliance
Lightning Source LLC
Chambersburg PA
CBHW051659090426
42736CB00013B/2453